ADVANCE PRAISE FOR *THE PAST AS PILGRIMAGE*

*The Past as Pilgrimage* is a bold call to recover a distinctly Catholic historical imagination and to chart an alternative conception of the historian's craft— one that views historical inquiry as much more than a professional enterprise. Shannon and Blum's manifesto will challenge and inspire historians who find Enlightenment historiography impoverished. And it will surely anger others for whom a different understanding of the historian's craft is unthinkable.

*- Donald Yerxa*
*Editor,* Fides et Historia

Taking as their starting point Alasdair MacIntyre's understanding of the inescapably tradition-grounded character of all forms of knowledge and moral inquiry, the authors argue that it is high time to look past the stale and exhausted forms into which so much professional historical writing has settled. Instead they seek to restore the dignity and scope of historical writing by envisioning it a kind of pilgrimage, a way of deepening and keeping faith with the common life of the Church. A provocative and reverent book, which deserves a very wide readership.

*- Wilfred M. McClay*
*Blankenship Chair in the History of Liberty*
*University of Oklahoma*

The authors show that all history is written from a particular worldview, and when the Catholic worldview is precluded, other philosophical or covertly theological perspectives take its place—much to the detriment of the Church, which depends upon historical narratives for its communal flourishing. Exhibiting the wise judgment, erudition about the past, and narrative skills that comprise good historical writing, this gem of a book offers a brilliant fresh start for Catholic historians. Future historians will point to this book as a classic text that accomplished for the field of history what MacIntyre accomplished for philosophy. A must read.

*- Matthew Levering*
*Perry Family Foundation Professor of Theology*
*Mundelein Seminary*

D1329929

Shannon and Blum argue that Christian historians need to rethink how they perform their craft, less subject to positivism and isolated from other disciplines, and more attuned to the big questions. Throughout they remain attentive to their responsibilities as both researchers and teachers. They are passionate about their thesis, will surely provoke a range of responses, but have added an important voice to the debate about the vocation of the Christian historian.

*- Rev. James L. Heft, S.M.*
*Alton Brooks Professor of Religion*
*President, Institute for Advanced Catholic Studies at*
*the University of Southern California*


Drawing on Catholic thinkers ranging from Augustine and Newman to Balthasar and MacIntyre, Shannon and Blum challenge the dogmas and functionally atheistic methodologies that shape most contemporary historical work. In doing so, they underscore the importance of a crucial and often neglected intellectual task: rescuing the writing of history from the delusion that we can provide an account of the past, our own and all humanity's, without reference to God.

*- Michael Baxter*
*Visiting Associate Professor, Catholic Studies*
*DePaul University*

# THE PAST AS PILGRIMAGE

# The Past as Pilgrimage

## NARRATIVE, TRADITION, AND THE RENEWAL OF CATHOLIC HISTORY

Christopher Shannon

Christopher O. Blum

Christendom Press
2014

Shannon, Christopher, 1962-

The past as pilgrimage : narrative, tradition, and the renewal of Catholic history / Christopher Shannon, Christopher O. Blum. -- Front Royal, VA : Christendom Press, 2014.

pages ; cm.

ISBN: 978-0-931888-47-2 (hardcover) ; 978-0-931888-01-4 (pbk.)

Includes bibliographical references and index.

1. Historians--Religious aspects--Catholic Church. 2. Christian historians--Objectivity. 3. MacIntyre, Alasdair C.--Influence. 4. Historiography--Religious aspects--Catholic Church. 5. Catholic Church--Historiography. 6. Learning and scholarship --Religious aspects--Catholic Church. 7. Religion and the humanities. I. Blum, Christopher Olaf, 1969- II. Title.

BX946 .S43 2014

282.09--dc23

1410

Published in the United States by:
Christendom Press
134 Christendom Drive
Front Royal, VA 22630
www.christendom.edu/press

*Cover image: Bartolome Esteban Murillo,* The Flight into Egypt *(c. 1647/50)*
*© Detroit Institute of Arts, Bridgeman Images*
*Cover design by Genevieve Bishop and Kelly Cole*

Manufactured in the United States of America

# Contents

# *Acknowledgments*

THE BOOK THAT WE present here is a reflection on the nature of Catholic scholarship that has grown out of years of working in small institutions that emphasize teaching over research. Thus, our greatest debt of gratitude goes to our colleagues and students at the Augustine Institute, Christendom College, and The Thomas More College of Liberal Arts.

The following individuals have contributed more directly to the reflections that follow: Michael Aeschliman, Anthony Andres, Dominic A. Aquila, Kathleen Blum, Glen Coughlin, John Fea, Jay Green, Brad Gregory, Ray Haberski, Reinhard Huetter, Tom Jodziewicz, Stephen M. Krason, Tim Lacy, Elisabeth Lasch-Quinn, Matthew Levering, Mark Lowery, Gene McCarraher, Wilfred M. McClay, Eric Miller, Glenn W. Olsen, Brennan Pursell, John Quinn, Paul Radzilowski, Kevin Schmiesing, David R. Stone, Fr. Paul Sullins, Adam Tate, Walter J. Thompson, Joseph A. Varacalli, Mark Weiner, Ronald A. Wells, Daniel Wickberg, Robert Louis Wilken, and Donald A. Yerxa. By hosting lectures, providing scholarly venues for publication, organizing roundtable exchanges, and providing critical feedback, these individuals have all helped us to think more deeply about the range of issues that we address in this book. They are a living witness to the persistence of the idea of a true community of scholars in an age otherwise characterized by impersonal professionalization.

Finally, this book would not exist without the support and hard work of the people at Christendom Press. We would like to thank in a special way Ken Ferguson, Executive Vice President of Christendom College, for his commitment to keeping the Press a voice for the Catholic intellectual tradition. Andrew Beer, Director and Editor in Chief of Christendom Press, and Kara Beer of American Philanthropic provided indispensable editorial support through repeated, careful readings of the manuscript. It is a much better book for their work. The authors, of course, take full blame for the deficiencies that may remain.

Christopher Shannon
*Front Royal, Virginia*

Christopher O. Blum
*Denver, Colorado*

*August 2014*

# *Preface*

LAMENTING THE "MASSIVE AMNESIA" that characterizes our time, Pope Francis observed that the "question of truth" is a "question of memory, deep memory, for it deals with something prior to ourselves" (*Lumen Fidei*, #25). There is a paradox here. Our age is characterized by an obsession with history, yet we have no "deep memory." History cannot fail to provide the matter for our conversations: the future is blank, the present fleeting, and the human things that so fascinate us today all lie in the past. And the font of our discourse is never-failing: channels, webpages, videos, museums, and commemorations of all kinds multiply beyond counting, to say nothing of historical monographs from university presses. Yet Catholics cannot be satisfied with mere talk, for they have been warned that "on the day of judgment men will render account for every careless word they utter" (Matt. 12:36). In our speech about the past, as in our actions generally, we are subject to the high standard of "redeeming the time" (Eph. 5:16). That we live amidst a crisis of truth is a fact beyond questioning. If, indeed, that crisis of truth has one of its roots in a crisis of memory, then historians in particular are called to reflect upon how their craft may best serve in this hour of need.

The two writers of this work belong to the generation of Catholic scholars that came of age in the decade following the publication of Alasdair MacIntyre's *After Virtue* (1981). To navigate the obstacles of graduate training with MacIntyre's critique of the forms of contemporary academic life in mind was, certainly, a help to understanding the experience, but it was also a challenge, in the sense of a gauntlet thrown down. With this essay, we are attempting to pick up that gauntlet, by presenting as an invitation to further reflection the results of our own experiences as Catholic historians and educators. Much like Brad S. Gregory's *Unintended Reformation* (Harvard University Press, 2012), a work similarly indebted to MacIntyre, this essay rests upon the premise that contemporary historical practice is in need of renewal, and perhaps most especially among Catholic historians. Although there continue to be isolated works of history that embody the virtue of right judgment that we here contend is the historian's standard, on the whole, there is neither a school, nor a professional organization, nor even a recognized movement of Catholic historiography that exists to promote reflection and conversation about the past for the sake of renewing Catholic life today. Nor has there been a sustained discussion of the virtues and practices of the Catholic intellectual life to match the seriousness with which Evangelicals have taken George M. Marsden's *Outrageous Idea of Christian Scholarship* (Oxford University Press, 1998). Our work intends to promote just such a conversation, at least initially among historians, but, we hope, also among Catholic educators and writers of all kinds.

The book that follows is concerned with the practice of Catholic historians as artisans of narrative and not with the faith-commitments of any actual Catholic historians. We have no desire to impose any more strict limits upon the meaning of Catholic than those offered by the Magisterium of the Church. All of the reflections that follow take the Catholic faith as a starting point, not as something to be argued about. We understand ourselves to be offering a proposal about the historian's craft as practiced by Catholics, not the practice of Catholics who happen to be historians.

The structure of the book is as follows. In the Introduction, we establish that historical narratives played an essential role in upholding the common good in past Christian communities. In the first chapter, we examine the last century of professional historiography in American universities in order to offer a critique of the dominant mode of Catholic historiography today. In the second, we provide an account of the historian's craft within the context of the Catholic intellectual tradition, arguing that the cultivation of the virtue of judgment is the historian's essential contribution to Catholic community life. The third and fourth chapters, respectively, treat a contemporary writer whom we take to embody the virtue of right judgment and the proper understanding of the end of Catholic history: Eamon Duffy and Pope Benedict XVI. In the Conclusion, we make some concrete suggestions about the path forward from the principles and examples we have discussed.

We understand this work to be an essay in the literal sense of the word. Although the discussions that follow do rest upon our previously published scholarly works, they are more essentially founded upon another kind of scholarship, the learning that comes from interpreting the past to students and popular audiences. It is our earnest hope that the work will be taken in the manner in which it is offered, which is as an argument about what Catholic history once was and might be again. As befits a book written by historians and for those who think that history has a vital role to play in the transmission of humane culture, there are numerous narrative segments within the work. On the whole, however, it is a statement of principles and, in that regard, an aspiration.

With all this in mind, let us be clear that what follows is not a history of the Catholic approach to history. Such a study could be useful and informative, but would likely serve only to reproduce the very narrative structures we seek to call into question. History is not progress, nor decline, nor a dialectical struggle of progress and decline. It is, rather, the story of man seeking Jesus Christ and, more importantly, Jesus Christ seeking man. We have tried to capture the nature of this two-fold search through the traditional image of pilgrimage. "God writes straight with crooked lines." So goes the proverb of disputed provenance, sometimes attributed to St. Augustine. If traditional pilgrimages have clearly defined routes, not so for the larger pilgrimage of history—and historical thinking—that we wish to address in this book. Beyond a clearly marked beginning and end in the person of Jesus Christ, the pilgrimage of history has as many routes as there are persons and cultures within the Church, understood as the Body of Christ moving through time. The journey toward a proper understanding of the place of historical thinking in the Catholic intellectual tradition has, for the last two hundred or so years, more nearly resembled a wandering in the desert than a pilgrimage proper. Still, even in the desert, the Lord made his presence felt. In the end, He led His people home.

# INTRODUCTION

## *Stories to Uphold the Good*

IT WAS ON THE eve of the Second World War that T. S. Eliot brought to a close his editorship of the quarterly review the *Criterion*. Looking out upon the "demoralization of society," a phenomenon he elsewhere identified with the recrudescence of paganism, Eliot's mood was one of resignation. Compared to Europe's spiritual malaise, the declining literary standards of the day—his particular concern as a poet—seemed a mere symptom. Much more grave was the inner disease, the lack of the coherent political philosophy and theological vision which alone could revivify and redirect European society. With the *Criterion*, Eliot had attempted to articulate just such a shared conception of European civilization by bringing together contributors from every major European country and from a wide variety of religious and philosophical perspectives for the sake of a common exploration of the good life. Characteristic of Eliot's endeavor was his decision to publish essays by both Jacques Maritain and Charles Maurras, two writers irrevocably divided by the condemnation of the *Action Française* in 1925, but who, to Eliot, represented strands of thought that were both sorely needed. By 1939, however, such efforts seemed too small and too late, and so a fatigued Eliot admitted that his own creativity was on the wane. His meditation upon the future of European learning was elegiac: "For this immediate future, perhaps for a long way ahead, the continuity of culture may have to be maintained by a very small number of people indeed—and these not necessarily the best equipped with worldly advantages." The task of keeping "critical thought alive" would fall, he surmised, to "small and obscure papers and reviews," hardly read "by anyone but their own contributors." A sober diagnosis, to be sure, but not a despairing one. For Eliot's valediction ended on a hopeful note, as he bore witness to his gratitude for the "associations, friendships and acquaintanceships of inestimable value" that had been brought about by the work of the *Criterion*.[1] His readers did not need to be reminded that among causes of the good, none is more efficacious than friendship.

Now some seventy years later and on the far shore of a vast cultural divide, we are keenly aware that what elements of the classical and Christian inheritance we have received have come to us by way of the thin and sinuous strands of cultural transmission Eliot foretold: from journals and books recommended by word-of-mouth or happened upon in libraries, from institutions and associations marginalized within or struggling outside of the mainstream academy, and especially from the wisdom and goodness of friends and mentors, themselves links in the living chain of tradition. We are also aware that we possess this inheritance but partially. Our knowledge of it suffices to teach us that we have been able to receive only some of its riches. When we compare ourselves to our own teachers who enjoyed a more integral formation and especially to the masters who have preceded us all, it becomes plain that we are not the measure, but the measured. To Augustine and Bede, to Boethius and Basil, to Newman and St. Paul we look as servants to the hands of their masters and as children to their elders.

Yet like Eliot, we too have been nourished by the hope that grows in the soil of friendship and common labor. We are part of and have helped to teach a new generation of students who have been drawn on by the inherent loveliness of truth and by the grace of Christ. We have participated in the clearing of land, the excavation and relaying of foundations, the opening of old attics, and the rediscovery of ancient

---

1. T. S. Eliot, "Last Words," *The Criterion* 18 (1939): 269–75. On the return of paganism, see "The Idea of a Christian Society," in T. S. Eliot, *Christianity and Culture* (New York: Harcourt, 1949), 14–19.

treasures. And we have begun to build. For to our generation, it seems, there falls a labor of recovery: of searching and sifting, of testing and of holding fast. There is a new creativity and courageous fashioning of things that not so long ago were abandoned as retrograde and moribund. All around us, hidden from the luster of the world, are studios for painting icons and farm fields reclaimed from waste, prayers sung in Latin and loaves of bread made by hand, small classes for the study of ancient languages, and campfires around which old folk songs are learned anew. And undergirding all this artistry and study is the first creativity of family life: a recommitment of men and women to the adventure and romance of fruitful Christian marriage.

Christian civilization has long been characterized by just such creative efforts of imitation and recovery; Charlemagne's use of the stones of Ravenna to build his chapel at Aachen and his imitation of Caesar in building a bridge over the Rhine, though stunning and very old examples, would be easy enough to multiply. Yet it does seem as though the task that we face today involves some peculiar difficulties thanks to the late date at which we are living and to the protean and anarchic culture we inhabit. The new communications media of the past two decades have only multiplied the already myriad possibilities for the idiosyncratic patching together of old and new in the name of tradition. It is plain that our labors of recovery stand particularly in need of consideration and understanding. Newman's reflection on this very point from the early days of the Oxford Movement seems even more relevant today:

> We have a vast inheritance, but no inventory of our treasures. All is given us in profusion; it remains for us to catalogue, sort, distribute, select, harmonize, and complete. We have more than we know how to use; stores of learning, but little that is precise and serviceable; Catholic truth and individual opinion, first principles and the guesses of genius, all mingled in the same works, and requiring to be discriminated. We meet with truths overstated or misdirected, matters of detail variously taken, facts incompletely proved or applied, and rules inconsistently urged or discordantly interpreted. . . . What we need at present

> for our Church's well-being, is not invention, nor originality, nor
> sagacity, nor even learning . . . but we need peculiarly a sound
> judgment, patient thought, discrimination, a comprehensive
> mind, an abstinence from all private fancies and caprices and
> personal tastes, in a word, Divine wisdom.[2]

In a similar vein, Alasdair MacIntyre has called for the cultivation of the "virtue of having an adequate sense of the traditions to which one belongs or which confront one." It is this virtue, a "kind of capacity for judgment," that we sorely need because it gives its possessor "a grasp of those future possibilities which the past has made available to the present."[3] It is a wisdom rooted in lived experience, operating upon the data of the past, for the sake of the future thriving of our communities. This virtue of judgment, we contend, is the quality or ability with respect to which the historian may most properly be called good or wise. It is the purpose of this essay to make that virtue better known and more available, so that Catholic historiography may become more fruitful and worthy of careful cultivation.

The attempt to identify and to delineate an authentic Catholic historiography involves three different kinds of arguments. First, we must distinguish our approach to the study of the past from history as it is currently practiced in the contemporary academy. Although this task is necessarily a critical one, it may also be regarded as furnishing the materials for a positive reconstruction of the historian's craft, for there is much to be valued in the practice of modern historians, even if some of the leading presuppositions of their practice need to be adjusted or even set aside. Second, we must engage the tradition we seek to serve and ask of it what role the historian can be called upon to play within the life of the Christian community and its search for the good. This task is itself both one of definition and one of retrieval and recovery; we are convinced that the current eclipse of historical stud-

---

2. John Henry Newman, *Apologia Pro Vita Sua*, ed. Ian Ker (London: Penguin, 1994), 76.

3. Alasdair MacIntyre, *After Virtue: A Study in Moral Theory*, 2nd edition (Notre Dame, IN: University of Notre Dame Press, 1984), 223.

ies within Christian intellectual life is a regrettable and temporary aberration. Third, we must provide evidence that the renewed historiography that we propose is an attainable, attractive, and promising endeavor, vital for the transmission of the faith and for the integrity of the life of faith seeking understanding.

Yet before any of these arguments can gain traction, we must first establish that our subject matter exists at all. We are contending that the historian's craft—the study of and reflection upon, and the writing, speaking, and teaching about the past—can play a significant role in the service of the common good. For we hold healthy communities, that is, communities constituted by living traditions and perpetuating themselves for future generations, to be communities sustained by narrative. This is the principle on which our argument turns, and so it is necessary to remove the suggestion that such a principle is mere paradox. We will do so by considering two examples of communal life so constituted and, in each case, do so through texts that display the art of true narrative—the historian's craft—employed for the sake of sustaining the virtues necessary for their community's thriving. When one looks to the Christian past, the difficulty lies not in finding communities constituted by tradition and sustained by narrative, but in choosing which ones to discuss. For reasons that will emerge in what follows, we will begin by considering the historian's craft in sermons preached in honor of St. Louis IX in the France of Louis XIV and Passions or martyrdom accounts from the earliest centuries of the Church.

## In Praise of the Great-Souled King

Christian identity was initially forged in opposition to political power. With the conversion of the Empire in the fourth century, the Church was faced with the need to articulate anew its relationship to rulers, and Christian identity, accordingly, took on a different hue. In the Latin West, the long and difficult age between the sack of Rome and the Crusades saw the steady deepening of a kind of Christian patriotism among peoples whose communal destiny was intimately bound to their Christian profession. And so, although John Paul II and Benedict XVI have both pointed to the martyrs and the early Church as the privileged locus of Christian memory and identity—while the liturgical prayer of the Church ceaselessly proclaims the same point—it is nevertheless useful to consider an example of the historical narrative from an age when the Christian faith was not understood to be in opposition to secular power. We will consider sermons preached in honor of St. King Louis IX by three orators of the age of Louis XIV: Esprit Fléchier, Louis Bourdaloue, and Jean-Baptiste Massillon.

To propose that these panegyrics be considered as examples of the historian's craft raises two immediate difficulties, one stemming from the nature of the genre and another from the complexion of the age in which they were composed. The last several decades of the seventeenth century seem to belong more to the nascent Enlightenment than to a living Christian culture. To take any artifacts from that era as evidence of healthy community seems problematic. Then there is the matter of the genre. How are works of formal oratory, panegyrics no less, to serve as an example for the historian's craft, a labor that requires dispassionate and disinterested analysis?

It would be perilous to suggest that the age of Louis XIV could serve as an uncomplicated example of a healthy Christian society. Many are the facets of French society during the *Grand Siècle* that have been criticized, both then and since, as imperfectly Christian or even essentially pagan. Yet it was also a century of saints. Merely to name them is to be astounded by the variety of their lives and of the different kinds of influence that they exercised in Europe and North America. Francis de Sales, Vincent de Paul, Jean de Brébeuf, Marie de l'Incarnation, Marguerite-Marie Alacoque, Jean Eudes, and Jean-Baptiste de la Salle are only the most prominent. It was also an age of imposing cultural achievement. To have given birth to Pascal, Racine, and Bossuet within the scope of a single century—let alone a decade and a half—is no mean achievement for a people, to say nothing of the contributions of Corneille and Marc-Antoine Charpentier, Fénelon and Georges de la Tour, André Le Nôtre and the Great Arnauld.

That such a parade of names can be readily assembled from

France's great century is itself instructive, for ages productive of genius are not necessarily the happiest. The changes experienced by the French between the Edict of Nantes and its revocation, between the age of Monsieur Vincent and that of the quarrels over Quietism and the papal bull *Unigenitus*, were almost seismic cultural shifts. This is an age in which the flowers of the Catholic reform growing from the Council of Trent bloomed amidst the thorns of the new way of life of the Enlightenment. An age in which a new world overseas was being evangelized while the French church was becoming deeply divided over the interpretation of the theology of St. Augustine. An age that was deeply traditional, and hierarchical in the fullest sense of the word, while being summoned to innovation by Descartes' *Discourse on Method* and inexorably transformed from within by an ambitious agenda of political consolidation. It was, in short, an era marked more by conflict and transformation than stability and repose. And though perhaps as much might be said of many eras, it seems as though France in the seventeenth century, and particularly in the century's latter half, was a laboratory for the testing of radically divergent visions of the good.[4] The historical writing and speaking of the day reflected that emerging cultural divide. Bossuet's *Discourse on Universal History*, for instance, was both a work of intellectual combat intended to counter the emerging threat of Spinozism as well as a textbook for the transmission of a Christian view of history.

In pointing to sermons preached on the feast of St. Louis as examples of the narrative art helping to sustain a community constituted by tradition, it should be understood that no golden age is being proposed, and that the sustaining we are going to consider is of goods that hang under the threats of attack and decay. No community is ever wholly lacking in foes, either external or internal. The very seriousness of the opposition to Christian society that in those days—whether in the lax morals of some of the Church's own members or

---

4. For an argument that Enlightenment should be understood to have been fully active by the latter part of the seventeenth century, see Jonathan I. Israel, *Radical Enlightenment: Philosophy and the Making of Modernity, 1650–1750* (New York: Oxford University Press, 2001).

in the clandestine works of philosophy produced by her opponents—was, however, at least a help in lending clarity of thought and expression to her defenders.

In the effort of preachers to buttress the moral fabric of Christian society in France, St. Louis IX (1214–70) was an especially useful model. To the refined Parisian listeners addressed by Fléchier, Bourdaloue, and Massillon, but also to broader audiences throughout the kingdom, St. Louis was the ideal Crusader who had sailed for Egypt and the Holy Land in the middle of his reign and then died in North Africa on a second crusade. The major turning points of his life were familiar: his coronation at the age of twelve, his victories over baronial uprisings during his early years as king, his acquisition of the Crown of Thorns and commissioning of the Sainte-Chapelle of Paris to hold it, his peace treaty with the English. Although his Crusades failed to attain their goal, St. Louis was nevertheless understood to have been a successful king according to the common standard of having bequeathed a well-knit kingdom to his son and having fathered a dynasty that would succeed him through the ages. After his canonization in 1297, his feast was celebrated locally on August 25 in parts of France, and widely enough in the fourteenth and fifteenth centuries that over four dozen sermons for the day survive in manuscript. It was not until the seventeenth century, however, that his feast was made obligatory throughout the realm as part of the work of consolidation undertaken after the wars of religion by Cardinal Richelieu and Louis XIII. The seventeenth century, in fact, witnessed a surge in devotion to St. Louis, resulting in the dedication of numerous churches to him and the publication of a spate of works of piety and erudition presenting him as a moral exemplar. Of these, the greatest by far in number were the sermons delivered on his feast day, enough of which remain to give a sense of the genre, both of its weaker representatives and of its solid successes.[5]

---

5. On the cult of St Louis in the medieval period, see M. Cecilia Gaposchkin, *The Making of Saint Louis: Kingship, Sanctity, and Crusade in the Later Middle Ages* (Ithaca, NY: Cornell University Press, 2008). For its growth in the seventeenth century, see Manfred Tietz, "Saint Louis Roi Chrétien: un mythe de la mission intéri-

These sermons were but one work of the resurgent Catholic piety of the two centuries following the Council of Trent, a piety whose manifestations were often highly choreographed, from the Forty-Hours Devotions staged by St. Francis de Sales to the classroom etiquette of the Brothers of Christian Schools.[6] It is sometimes difficult, therefore, to separate what was constructed or contrived from what might be thought sufficiently a matter of principle or true insight as to be perennial. Adding to the difficulty in assessing works produced in this age is the complexity of French culture during the reign of the Sun King: pagan symbolism and habits of mind coexisted in uneasy tension with Christianity, and worldly display sometimes got the better of Christian modesty and good sense. What was true of the stage and of the rostrum was at times also true of the pulpit: the temptation to indulge in sonorous language, high-flying rhetoric, and theatrics simply for their effect was real, and not always avoided. "The Christian discourse," lamented La Bruyère as the century waned, "has become a spectacle."[7] So when Jean Doujat, lawyer and sometime reader to the Dauphin, took the occasion of a speech in honor of St. Louis before the Académie Française to drift into saccharine flattery of Louis-le-Grand, his audience might have found the exercise wanting in taste, but they would have had no cause to have called it a novelty.[8] Nor

---

eure du XVIIième siècle," in *La Conversion au XVIIe siècle: actes du XIIe colloque de Marseille* (Marseille: Centre méridional de rencontres sur le XVIIe siècle, 1983), 59–69. A recent biography of St. Louis that gives lengthy consideration to the memory of him, by his biographer Joinville and by the French in general, is Jacques Le Goff, *Saint Louis* (Paris: Gallimard, 1996).

6. See Jill R. Fehleison, "Appealing to the Senses: The Forty Hours Celebrations in the Duchy of Chablais, 1597–98," *Sixteenth Century Journal* 36 (2005): 375–96. And for another striking example, see the description of the celebration of the canonization of Saints Ignatius Loyola and Francis-Xavier staged by in Antwerp in 1622, in Louis Chatellier, *The Europe of the Devout: The Catholic Reformation and the Formation of a New Society*, trans. Jean Birrell (Cambridge: Cambridge University Press, 1989), 52–55.

7. Jean de La Bruyère, *Les Caractères*, XV.1 (Paris: Librairie générale française, 1995), 557.

8. See Jean Doujat, "Discours prononcé à l'Académie Française pour la distribution des Prix le jour de saint Louis, 1681," in Pierre Zoberman, *Les Panégyriques*

were the sermons themselves immune from mistreatment. Speaking in 1649 at the church of San Luigi in Rome, Jean-Jacques Bouchard strayed into what has been called "an unrestrained celebration of the superiority of France, and especially of its capital."[9] Even when the preachers were more elevated and refined, they nevertheless made frequent reference to contemporary events—even to controversial ones such as the promulgation of the Four Articles of the Gallican church and the revocation of the Edict of Nantes—in such a way as to lay themselves open to the charge of being apologists for the Sun King's regime.[10] Where good French patriotism stops and pragmatic politics begins is difficult to say, for the kind of retelling of the French national myth that is present in Bossuet's funeral oration for Henriette-Marie of France, to name but one example, was certainly expected and, judging from that work's popularity, appreciated without much in the way of second thoughts.[11]

Sermon-going was a common practice in seventeenth-century Paris. To have heard a sermon by Bossuet or Bourdaloue in the morning and then to have seen the latest play by Racine in the afternoon would not have been impossible, especially for those of means. These tasteful men and women were exacting critics who knew what they were listening for in a sermon. As La Bruyère explained, they demanded that the preachers "keep to the beaten track, say what has been said before and what they expect him to say." Good preaching he thought to be rare, for though "the material is great . . . it is tired and overly-familiar; the principles are sure ones, but the auditors perceive the conclusions that follow from them at a glance."[12] It was a

du roi prononcés dans l'Académie Française (Paris: Presses de l'Université de Paris-Sorbonne, 1991), 185–89.

9. Thomas Worchester, S.J., "The Catholic Sermon," in *Preachers and People in the Reformations and Early Modern Period*, ed. Larissa Taylor (Leiden: Brill, 2001), 28–9.

10. See Tietz, "Saint Louis Roi Chrétien," 66.

11. See Jacques-Bénigne Bossuet, "Funeral Oration for Henriette-Marie de France, Queen of Great Britain," trans. C. O. Blum, *Faith and Reason* 29 (2004): 269–301.

12. La Bruyère, *Les Caractères*, XV.26, p. 567.

golden age of pulpit eloquence not from ease, but from adversity: the level of talent, piety, and learning in a few great preachers rose to the challenge of a most discriminating public. And the challenge was also a spiritual one, as Peter France has explained: "face to face with an audience of great worldliness and himself a participant in a ceremony which for most of those present was only nominally religious, the preacher was in an exposed position that might well demand considerable heart-searching and sacrifice of integrity."[13] It is precisely because their integrity was not sacrificed to the claims of effectiveness that the panegyrics of St. Louis preached by Fléchier, Bourdaloue, and Massillon stand out as works of lasting merit.

In writing his sermon on St. Louis, Esprit Fléchier (1632–1710), member of the *Académie Française* and later bishop of Nîmes, adhered to the form common to French classical oratory.[14] He began with an exordium that developed his chosen Biblical text into an explicit theme and then paused to invoke the Virgin Mary with the recitation of the *Ave Maria.* He then set out the main points of his oration in a brief section devoted to the division of the sermon into its parts—here three in number, but in other contemporary sermons often only two. In the body of the discourse he treated the points in order, and then brought the work to a close with a terse peroration, in which—again true to the common form—he exhorted his listeners to apply the lessons of the sermon to their own lives. Fléchier's oration, like those of Bourdaloue and Massillon, was of a length to admit of reading or recitation in about an hour, a length that suggests a comparison to the kind of address that prevails in academia today.

The competent speaker knows better than to try the patience of his audience with matters too widely known to bear a full rehearsal. Whether in a conference paper, a formal address, or the ineptly named

---

13. Peter France, *Rhetoric and Truth in France: Descartes to Diderot* (Oxford: Clarendon Press, 1972), 121.

14. See Peter Bayley, *French Pulpit Oratory, 1598–1650: A Study in Themes and Styles* (Cambridge: Cambridge University Press, 1980), 101–11, and Jacques Truchet, "La division en points dans les sermons de Bossuet," *Revue d'histoire littéraire de la France* 52 (1952): 316–29.

job-talk, professional historians today rarely resort to lengthy narratives. Just as professional, though in a different line, Fléchier not only refrained from retelling his subject's life in chronological order, he also passed lightly over its main events, as being known to all and requiring only to be called to mind for their significance to be pondered. The mere names of Taillebourg and Damietta sufficed to evoke the king's courage; the woods of Vincennes stood as an icon of his devotion to justice, the sands of Tunis of his perseverance and zeal. The difficulty facing the panegyrist of St. Louis was to make these well-known episodes to be more than nursery fables or patriotic pap. More, that is, than old news. Like the professional scholar who seeks to bring to light something in the past that contributes to the conversation taking place among living historians, the preacher scoured his material for something he might make use of for his present need. His task was to bring the king's life to bear upon the besetting sins and weaknesses of the age, and it was a task of judgment and argument, and of the marshalling of facts, not their bare enumeration.

As a young man, Fléchier had moved in the kind of social and literary circles that his contemporaries characterized as "worldly" (*mondain*).[15] By August of 1681, however, when he composed his sermon, he had embraced the devout life, and his panegyric impresses the reader as an instance of the social and spiritual idealism of the Catholic reform. As his Biblical text, he chose a passage from Proverbs (21:1): "The king's heart is a stream of water in the hand of the Lord; he turns it wherever he will." A king's heart, he explained, could be held in but one of three places: in his own hand, in the hands of his people, or in the hand of the Lord. The king who attempted to rule himself would end a slave to his passions: a bold opening for a sermon preached just two months after the sudden death–amidst rumors of poisoning–of Mademoiselle de Fontanges, whose health had never recovered from the difficult delivery of the most recent of Louis XIV's

---

15. On Fléchier, see Jean Calvet, *La littérature religieuse en France de François de Sales à Fénélon* (Paris: Les Editions Mondiales, 1956), 333–34.

burgeoning brood of bastards.[16] The king ruled by his people would be as weak and vacillating as their transitory moods and factions. Only the king whose heart was in the hand of God would be a fitting instrument of divine justice and mercy, as St. Louis, the devout king, had been.

The division of the sermon into its three parts proceeded directly from this theme. St. Louis had placed his heart in the Lord's hands, and the Lord had fashioned it so as to preserve it from those faults and temptations so common among the great. To keep him from disordered self-love, the Lord gave him "a heart tender towards his people." To preserve him from the illusion of independence, the Lord gave him "a self-controlled heart." And to inoculate him against the "spirit of the world," the Lord gave him "a heart submitted to and fervent towards God." Each of his three points set St. Louis's affections in opposition to the desires and attitudes prevailing among the *mondains*. Fléchier's mode of argumentation was Augustinian in content but Aristotelian in form: he would heighten the praise of his hero's right desire by displaying the contrast with the perverse desires of a society saturated with public professions of the Christian virtues, but less impressive in the living of them.[17]

"Kingship," the preacher affirmed, is not only a "rank," it is a "ministry," that is, an office of religion, justice, and charity. St. Louis, understanding the weightiness of the office to which his birth had called him, had prayed for wisdom like Solomon of old. God's grace then made of him "one of those great souls destined to oppose the pride and the rebellion of men." A number of powerful barons, led by Pierre Mauclerc, duke of Brittany and a royal cousin, took the occasion of the Queen-regent's unpopularity to risk an uprising against the crown and even enter into an alliance with Henry III of England. Not only did St. Louis—or rather, his loyal nobles—defeat the rebellion, but afterwards, when ruling in his own name at the age of

---

16. See Georges Couton, *La chair et l'âme: Louis XIV entre ses maîtresses et Bossuet* (Grenoble: Presses universitaires de Grenoble, 1995), 155–84.

17. See Aristotle, *Rhetoric*, I.9, especially 1368a19 and following.

twenty, he accorded Mauclerc a complete pardon. The rebels were not greeted with "coolness," but instead were "looked upon as new-found friends" and employed in the king's "holy expeditions," the Crusades of 1239 and 1248.[18] "Clemency, justice, generosity, loyalty, and courage shown in dangers to the community," were the qualities singled out by the master of orators, Cicero, as "pleasing to hear about in laudatory speeches."[19] But Fléchier was not merely responding to what the art required, he was placing St. Louis in opposition to the contemporary cult of honor. "Where can we find such sincere and magnanimous hearts today?" he asked. "Never have men been so punctilious nor so delicate; we take offense at everything, and we never consent to be offended with impunity."[20] The mania for dueling had been dealt a severe blow by Richelieu and Louis XIII, but the disorders in the cult of honor that had supported the custom remained to be rooted out.

St. Louis's heart had been made tender towards his subjects, and though the barons of the realm were surely the most difficult to love, they were by no means the most needy. It was to his common subjects, and especially to the poor, that the king was particularly devoted. In turning to this characteristic of St. Louis, the preacher invited his audience to savor with him the well-known image: "How I love to imagine this good king, as history represents him, in the wood of Vincennes, under those trees hallowed by time, stopping for awhile amidst his innocent recreation [*divertissemens*—Fléchier's spelling] to listen to the complaints and to receive the requests of his subjects." Indeed, the story, as Joinville relates it, is a winning one, and Fléchier allowed himself to be moved by the retelling of it, making a rare foray into sonority, and delighting, good patriot that he was, in the praise of a king who had "rendered his judgments without delay and his advice with authority, with equity, with tenderness; king, judge, and father all in one." Yet again, the need of his audience was paramount, and he drove

---

18. Esprit Fléchier, "Panégyrique de Saint Louis," in *Oeuvres complètes de Fléchier* (Paris: Boisle fils ainé, Berquet, Dufour, 1827), IV: 290–93.

19. Cicero, *On the Ideal Orator* (*De Oratore*), II.343, trans. James M. May and Jakob Wisse (New York: Oxford University Press, 2001), 217.

20. Fléchier, "Saint Louis," 293.

home his point with considerable emphasis. "What magistrate today," he abruptly asked, "wishes to interrupt his relaxation (*divertissemens*) when it is a matter, I do not say of the comfort, but of the honor, and perhaps even of the life of one of those miserable wretches?" Pascal's denunciation of the idleness and boredom of the rich had found a living voice in the preacher: "The time for pleasures has absorbed that of duties." "The magistrature is only too often a cover for idleness." The noble judges and lawyers of the Parlements had allowed their amusements to "become the sacred part of their lives which no one dares to bother." They did not measure up to the example of St. Louis, who "did not flee work in that way," but instead devoted himself "like the father of a family" to his poor subjects.[21]

In the second and third parts of his discourse, Fléchier continued to contrast the example of St. Louis with the lives of the great ones of his day. Against outward displays of pride (the Sun King was of course not mentioned, but hardly needed to be), he placed the example of St. Louis's humility in choosing to enter the conquered Egyptian city of Damietta as a penitent, walking barefoot in procession behind the Cross. Against the decadence of the court, that "land fertile in frivolous amusements, profane loves, and evil desires," he set the corporal mortifications voluntarily undertaken by the king as acts of penance. And against the disordered desire for greatness shown by kings and conquerors, he praised the "greatness of soul" that St. Louis had displayed by turning down the papal offer of the crown of the Holy Roman Empire. Finally, and at some length, Fléchier praised and gave illustrations of St. Louis's zeal for the Christian faith, setting his pious deeds in opposition to the characteristic vices of the day: "We have but the tincture and the sheen of religion; injuries done to God do not bother us. We dare not contradict impiety for fear of seeming to be censorious or hypocritical." In his day, St. Louis had "suppressed impiety, libertinism, and blasphemy by the severity of his edicts;" now, in the age of Louis XIV, his example would serve the same ends by encouraging the program of social renovation proposed earlier in the

---

21. Ibid.

century by St. Vincent de Paul and the Company of the Blessed Sacrament.[22] Abbé Fléchier's panegyric was indeed, as François-Xavier Cuche has observed, a "profoundly serious work" that aimed to offer a "model of sanctity for all."[23] The preacher had no time for royal flattery, grandiloquent narrative, or patriotic effusion. Nor would he offer fantastic tales of miracles, which were becoming less compelling to a more critical age.[24] His aim was rational persuasion: to make St. Louis "reign in the heart of the good French [*des bons François*], those who imitate his great examples."[25]

In contrast to the unornamented sermon preached by Fléchier, the panegyrics pronounced by Louis Bourdaloue and Jean-Baptiste Massillon were each significantly more grand. For Bourdaloue, preaching at the newly founded royal academy of St-Cyr, dedicated to the memory of St. Louis, a measure of grandiloquence was simply required.[26] Fresh in his own mind, if not that of his audience, was his own funeral oration for the Prince de Condé, whom four months earlier he had praised as a "hero predestined by God" and a model of Christian magnanimity.[27] A less inspiring St. Louis would never do. So the preacher chose the text "*magnificus in sanctitate*" and made a compelling case for both the holiness and the greatness of his soul. Massillon, preaching in Paris, set himself against the influence of the

---

22. Fléchier, "Saint Louis," 300–8, 311. On the Company of the Blessed Sacrament, see Henry Phillips, *Church and Culture in Seventeenth-Century France* (Cambridge: Cambridge University Press, 1997), 20–23.

23. François-Xavier Cuche, "Le Panégyrique de Saint Louis de Fléchier," in Emmanuèle Lesne-Jaffro, ed., *Fléchier et les Grand Jours d'Auvergne*, volume 122 of the series Biblio 17 (Tübingen: Gunter Narr, 2000), 93–114.

24. On the "crisis of hagiography" following the rise of critical historiography that shaped the composition of panegyrics in the later seventeenth century, see Jacques Truchet, *Bossuet Panégyriste* (Paris: Cerf, 1962), 24–32.

25. Fléchier, "Saint Louis," 316.

26. See Bruno Neveu, "Du culte de Saint Louis à la glorification de Louis XIV: la maison royale de Saint-Cyr," *Journal des savants* (1988): 277–90.

27. Louis Bourdaloue, "Oraison funèbre de Louis de Bourbon, Prince de Condé," in *Œuvres de Bourdaloue* (Paris : Lefèvre, 1834), III:65. The funeral oration was preached on April 26, 1687. The sermon on St. Louis at St.-Cyr followed on September 4.

theater, then steadily gaining ground as a rival to the Church's cultural authority.[28] He followed Bourdaloue's line of argument, but not his style, producing a rounded Ciceronian oration which offered his hearers a choice between the eloquence of the stage and that of the pulpit.

The Jesuit Bourdaloue (1632–1704) brought to his sermon the readiness for spiritual combat that characterized the spirituality of Ignatius Loyola. His task was to challenge the belief that there were "conditions in the world that were absolutely contrary to holiness." In every age, the worldly have "supposed that evangelical perfection, because of its essential ties to humility, renders men incapable of great deeds." Yet in "these last centuries" the error has been renewed by "a false sage," who has found followers in the "infinite number of the libertine and impious" who call themselves by the name of "politique."[29] To have named Montaigne as his foe would scarcely have been more direct. Montaigne's *Essays*, as Marc Fumaroli has noted, were "read and reread" throughout the century "as the 'gentleman's psalter,' the antidote to servility and false piety."[30] For Bourdaloue, the significance of the doctrine of the "false sage" lay not in its novelty, but in its universality: it was the voice of the natural man seeking to make his way without the assistance of divine grace or the light of the Gospel. To be content with "worldly grandeur," he admonished, was to risk "losing humility and zeal for religion" and to fall into a self-love that extends even to the point of shrugging off "the yoke of penitence and Christian austerity."[31] Hard words, perhaps, to apply to one so moderate as Montaigne, but, whether identified with him or not, certainly

---

28. See Phillips, *Church and Culture in Seventeenth-Century France*, 59–65.

29. Bourdaloue, "Sermon pour la fête de Saint Louis, roi de France," in *Œuvres de Bourdaloue* (Paris: Lefèvre, 1834), II: 638, 643.

30. Fumaroli, *Le Poète et le Roi: Jean de La Fontaine en son siècle* (Paris: Editions de Fallois, 1997), 30. The phrase "gentleman's psalter," or *bréviaire des honnêtes gens*, was coined by Jacques Davy Cardinal du Perron; see Alan Boase, *The Fortunes of Montaigne: A History of the* Essays *in France, 1580–1669* (1935; New York: Octagon Books, 1970), 312.

31. Bourdaloue, "Saint Louis," 643, 639.

the very reverse of the devout life envisioned by St. Francis de Sales and the Catholic reform.[32]

Against the threat of cynicism and sloth, Bourdaloue pitted the example of the magnanimous saint: determined and courageous in his pursuit of the ideal of holiness. His sermon as a whole was one long argument from example to prove that the conjunction "*magnificus in sanctitate*" was not self-defeating, first by setting forth the evidence of St. Louis's heroic sanctity, and then by demonstrating the greatness of his kingship. Like Fléchier, Bourdaloue did not supply a narrative. His examples were briefly set forth, a few words sufficing to prove each of the leading characteristics of St. Louis's character: humility, zeal for the Christian faith, tireless charity, and stern asceticism. The achievements of his reign were likewise adduced with a brevity possible only before an audience that shared a common understanding with the speaker. Unlike Fléchier and Massillon, Bourdaloue did not permit himself lengthy digressions to paint the troubled morals of his day, preferring instead to teach through his subject, as when he described the austerity and moral rigor that St. Louis imposed upon his court. Compared to the others, however, Bourdaloue did allow himself colorful words, making free use of magnificent, heroic, and great, and concluding with a sumptuous prayer that the reigning king might enjoy the protection of his heavenly patron. But this was merely so much gilt framing a portrait as stark as a La Tour or a Rembrandt. For Bourdaloue, trained as a scholastic, knew the difference between delighting and convincing, and his task was to impress a single conclusion upon the minds of his auditors through two complementary hypothetical arguments. If holiness could be attained even on a royal throne, then holiness could be attained in "every state of life and rank," and if holiness could secure greatness in a king, then it could be no bar to the attainment of any true excellence. But St. Louis was at once a great king and a great saint. His example, therefore, sufficed to prove that "there is no worldly condition in which one cannot be a

---

32. On Montaigne's status among the free-thinkers of the seventeenth century, see Giovanni Dotoli, *Montaigne et les libertins* (Paris: Honoré Champion, 2006), and Philippe Desan, "Le libertinage des Essais," *Montaigne Studies* XIX (2007): 17–28.

Christian, and a perfect one," nor is there anything other than "holiness that can give to us a solid perfection" in whatever position in the world we occupy.[33]

Massillon (1663–1742), educated and formed by the Oratorians, had the same end in view as Bourdaloue, but took the opposite approach to his craft. He, too, divided his treatment into two parts, but reversed Bourdaloue's order, first setting out to prove that St. Louis's "holiness made him a great king," and then showing how his "royalty made him a great saint." He eschewed the austere tool of Bourdaloue's logic, and instead employed his quill as a conductor's baton to produce a sweeping composition that sought to convince by its high tone.[34] Fléchier and Bourdaloue had restricted themselves narrowly to the king's personal achievements and had noted them with economy. Massillon was more ample. In his sermon we meet Blanche of Castile and Robert de Sorbon, hear narrative passages on the baron's revolt and St. Louis's burial of dead crusaders, and, most significantly, are asked to understand St. Louis by comparison to the heroes of old: Abraham and Moses, the kings David and Clovis, and the Emperor Theodosius. And all of this was presented in a cadence that emphasized the dignity of the subject:

> The holy king's piety and humanity made for the happiness of his people. Accessible to all, he would deprive not even the least of his subjects the pleasure of looking upon his sovereign. He always presented them with a smiling countenance, tempering the majesty of the throne by his affability, and, like Moses, draping a veil of sweetness and moderation over the brilliance of his person and office, so that the minds of those who approached him might be made calm; and he stripped himself of all pomp and grandeur, so that those coming upon him could hardly perceive that he was the master until he accorded his favor.[35]

33. Bourdaloue, "Saint Louis," 643, 646.

34. On Massillon's willingness to appeal to the emotions, see J. Patrick Lee, "Voltaire and Massillon: Affinities of the Heart," *French Review* 50 (1977): 437–45.

35. Jean-Baptiste Massillon, "Sermon pour le jour de saint Louis, roi de France," *Oeuvres complètes de Massillon* (Paris: Raymond, 1821), IX:219–60. Truchet notes

The orator not only named the king's magnanimity, he also suggested it by the tones of his voice.

Massillon's sermon was ranged against the cultural influence of the stage. Accordingly it was the king's "vigilance," that he chose to set in opposition to the "softness" and "luxury" of "that sumptuous city," Louis XIV's Paris, with the "lascivious pomp of its theaters and spectacles." St. Louis had also lived in a Paris threatened by those "public academies of lubricity," the "impure theaters." By his appointment of "new men" chosen for their incorruptibility as judges, St. Louis had succeeded in reestablishing the "well-being of public morals" by seeing that the "impure theaters were overturned." The preacher's pitch rose and became almost shrill as he named "the spectacles, the dangers of which we today find it so hard to convince you, in spite of all of the rules of the faith" and "the comedians, whom even those of the highest rank do not blush today to honor with their familiarity." His St. Louis was a counter-example to error, just as Bourdaloue's had been, but his rival was Molière instead of Montaigne. The great comic had made a career out of opposing the despotic moralism of devout fathers with the suave moderation of his heroes and heroines.[36] Massillon's response to Molière's brand of insinuation was frankly to admit the problem of hypocrisy among Christian fathers and to point to St. Louis as an exemplar to be imitated and as proof that parental probity was possible. This point was the sermon's very crux. For those "public duties" that St. Louis fulfilled so faithfully are made less difficult by the "brilliance that surrounds them," whereas in the "constant practice of those hidden and ordinary duties" one is less likely to remain "on guard against oneself." It is in the family, therefore, that "solid virtue chiefly appears."[37] In spite of his ornamented rhetoric, Massillon's message was in keeping with the sobriety of contemporary French piety: the responsible Christian is to set aside the fantasies of the stage

---

that Massillon did not normally devote much space to narration; see Bossuet, *Panégyriste*, 40–41.

36. See Antony McKenna, *Molière: Dramaturge Libertin* (Paris: Honoré Champion, 2005).

37. Massillon, "Saint Louis," 255.

and work out his salvation by fulfilling the ordinary duties of the state in life in which Providence has placed him.[38]

These three sermons are examples of how the art of true narrative can help to sustain a community constituted by tradition. As works of historical narrative, they are, we have noted, of a peculiar kind. They are arguments or appeals spoken within the context of a shared historical understanding, and, as such, they are more closely related to the formal academic speech than to the other common works of the historian's craft. Unlike the academic speech, however, the historical understanding that they presupposed was not shared only by a professional association, but by the larger political and ecclesial community to which the preachers belonged. Whether we understand the France of Louis XIV as coming at the end of the "age of eloquence" or at the beginning of the "age of conversation," it was certainly an age of polished speech and ritual performance, an age—even a golden age—of theater and oratory, an age when beliefs and convictions were enacted and not merely written down.[39] In that age, good orators were celebrated for their skill: fashionable churches secured the famous preachers for series of sermons at Advent and Lent; favorite sermons were preached and preached again, with their titles advertised on broadsheets; footmen were dispatched to save good seats for their masters and mistresses.[40] No mere celebrity, however, the

---

38. Compare Pierre Nicole, *Traité de la Comédie* (1675), ed. Georges Couton (Paris: Les Belles Lettres, 1961).

39. See Marc Fumaroli, *L'Age de l'éloquence: rhétorique et 'res literaria' de la Renaissance au seuil de l'époque classique* (1980; Paris: Albin Michel, 1994), and Benedetta Craveri, *The Age of Conversation*, trans. Teresa Waugh (New York: New York Review of Books, 2005).

40. On preaching in the seventeenth century, and especially in France, see Jean Calvet, *La littérature religieuse en France de François de Sales à Fénélon* (Paris : Del Duca, 1956), 321–37; François Bluche, *La vie quotidienne au temps de Louis XIV* (Paris: Hachette, 1984), 102–7; Manuel Morán and José Andrés-Gallego, "The Preacher," in Rosario Villari, ed., *Baroque Personae*, trans. Lydia G. Cochrane (Chicago: University of Chicago Press, 1995), 126–59; and Joris Van Eijnatten, "Reaching Audiences: Sermons and Oratory in Europe," in *The Cambridge History of Christianity, volume VII: Enlightenment, Reawakening, and Revolution, 1660–1815*, eds. Stewart J. Brown and Timothy Tackett (Cambridge: Cambridge University Press, 2006), 128–46.

preacher occupied a privileged cultural role. Delivering his sermons within the context of the Church's annual liturgical cycle, he was the interpreter of a universal history that encompassed both the drama of salvation and the growth and development of the French nation. The Church was the mistress of her feast days, suppressing the extraneous and retaining those—even comparatively new ones such as the feast of St. Louis—whose catechetical function outweighed the dangers of idleness and drunken revelry.[41] For the preacher who sought to fulfill the Tridentine ideal of sacred eloquence, the subject of St. Louis presented an ideal combination: a well-loved saint whose life was a portrait of a high moral ideal consistently striven for and attained. He was a Frenchman of whom even the dourest Jansenist could be proud. St. Francis de Sales, who was particularly devoted to his memory, was led to exclaim "O happy France" when meditating upon the blessing of such a wise king.[42] And the model sermons on St. Louis collected by the abbé Houdry at the turn of the eighteenth century bear witness that other preachers on St. Louis were scarcely less enthusiastic.[43]

Although it is unnecessary to dwell upon the fact that a common piety for a father-figure such as St. Louis helps to unite a political community, it is worth stressing that the sermons we have considered were not merely expressions of the French patriotic myth. Nor were they fables embroidered with accounts of fantastic miracles. They were direct appeals to mind and heart for the sake of encouraging the pursuit of the virtues in the face of temptation and of rival accounts of the human good. The particular struggle of the day was between a certain worldly moderation, often referred to as honnêteté (uprightness, civility, or good breeding), and a fully Christian conception of the human person perfected by grace. "The only thing talked about in those days," as Jean Calvet put it, "at the theater, from the

---

41. See J. Maarten Ultee, "The Suppression of Fêtes in France, 1666," *Catholic Historical Review* 62 (1976): 181–99.

42. See "Plan d'un panégyrique de saint Louis, roi de France," (1602) in *Oeuvres de St. François de Sales*, ed. B. Mackey, O.S.B. (Annecy: Niérat, 1896), 7: 467–68.

43. See Vincent Houdry, *La Bibliothèque des Prédicateurs*, nouvelle édition, (Paris: Adolphe Josse, 1869), XVI: 324–78.

pulpit, in the salons and in the books of the moralists was worldly virtue (*la vertu mondaine*), the kind that could be achieved by following the sentiment of honor alone, without the help of God."[44] There was, in fact, a new paganism on the rise across the seventeenth century, perceptible in such phenomena as the use of Julian the Apostate as a model of virtue and the paintings of Apollo in the "wholly secular shrine" that was Louis XIV's throne room at Versailles.[45] Amidst such an atmosphere, the preachers' "appeal to St. Louis," as Manfred Tietz observed, "clearly expressed the complete refusal of the new secularized vision of a world that no longer found its values and its models in the Christian tradition of the country, but instead in the cult of pagan antiquity."[46] If it is the task of the historian to contest rival interpretations of the past, and to do so with warmth and vigor when he thinks that principles crucial to the well-being of his community are at stake, then the sermons on St. Louis by Fléchier, Bourdaloue, and Massillon are indeed worthy examples of the historian's craft.

A critic might reasonably question whether these examples, however worthy, are living models for historians writing in the twenty-first century. Contemporary dramatists may admire Shakespeare, but few if any would desire, much less dare, to hold themselves accountable to the traditional standards of Elizabethan prosody. If contemporary fiction writers, who claim absolute autonomy in their aesthetic choices, cannot in good conscience choose to write as practitioners of a traditional literary form, so much greater the challenge for historians. The last two hundred years of literary development have seen fiction writers increasingly freed from all constraints of literary form, while developments in historical thinking and writing have imposed

---

44. Jean Calvet, "Introduction" to Madame de La Fayette, *La Princesse de Clèves* (Paris: Nelson, 1932), v.

45. On Julian the Apostate, see Montaigne, "On Freedom of Conscience," in *Essays*, II.19, 760–63, and François de La Mothe le Vayer, *La Vertue des Payens* (1641), in *Oeuvres de François de La Mothe Le Vayer*, nouvelle édition, tome V, partie I (Dresden: Michel Groeel, 1757), 385. On Versailles, see T. C. W. Blanning, *The Culture of Power and the Power of Culture: Old Regime Europe, 1660–1789* (Oxford: Oxford University Press, 2002), 37.

46. Tietz, "Saint Louis roi chrétien," 63.

increasingly stringent constraints on historians. The professional academic history that developed in the nineteenth century advanced a standard of empirical verifiability that would seem to consign premodern genres to the ash heap of historical writing. Can a modern historian responsibly approach a saint as anything other than a product of a certain historical moment? Can a modern historian approach the classic texts of hagiography as anything other than symptomatic of the sensibilities of a particular author or the needs of a particular community? After such knowledge, what history? To consider these questions, we will now turn to an even earlier tradition of historical reflection through the lives of saints, the narrative of the martyrdom of Perpetua and Felicity.

## Imitating Christ in his Death

Blessed John Henry Newman once remarked, "To be deep in history is to cease to be Protestant."[47] Newman has served as a guide of sorts for Catholic historical thinking across the spectrum of orthodoxy: conservatives defending orthodoxy may invoke his demonstration of the antiquity of the Church's truth claims, while liberals concerned to challenge orthodoxy may find a rationale for change in his notion of the development of doctrine over time. Both uses of his writings seem to miss the deeper meaning of Newman's insight into the link between history and faith. Catholics do not look to history simply to prove doctrine; rather, they look to the past for stories that help them understand their faith as a whole way of life. It is perhaps in this way that they remain most faithful to the spirit of the early Church. The early Church maintained its unity less in explicit assent to common doctrines than in shared liturgical practices.[48] These practices, most especially the Mass, told the story of the life, sacrificial death and

---

47. John Henry Newman, *An Essay on the Development of Christian Doctrine*, 6th edition (London, 1878; reprinted Notre Dame, IN: University of Notre Dame Press, 1989), 8.

48. Peter Brown, *The Cult of the Saints: Its Rise and Function in Latin Christianity* (Chicago: University of Chicago Press, 1981), 19.

glorious resurrection of Jesus Christ. Early Christians understood this story as not simply an event of the past nor a merely spiritual experience in the present, but as training for what Robin Darling Young has called the "quasi-eucharistic sacrifice of martyrdom."[49] Christians were to come to know Christ by imitating Christ—most especially in his sacrificial death. Though only a minority of Christians suffered actual martyrdom, the stories of the martyrs provided the foundation for a distinct, alternative Christian culture.

No historian would doubt the centrality of martyrdom to early Christian culture, yet most have been at pains to understand it as anything but the expression of love for Jesus Christ. Edward Gibbon continues to cast a long shadow on the secular historical imagination. The continued preference for the phrase "late antiquity" over "early Christianity" to frame the first centuries after Christ speaks to the secular orientation of much historical study of the period. Historians quick to dismiss Christian theology as a kind of "Platonism for the masses" have a tougher time explaining martyrdom, which had little if any precedent in Greco-Roman culture.[50] Seeking to downplay the historical uniqueness of Christianity, they have looked elsewhere in the ancient world—particularly to the Jewish tradition of resistance to pagan imperial authority from the time of the Maccabees in the second century B.C. In his classic study, *Martyrdom and Persecution in the Early Church*, W. H. C. Frend comes close to accounting Christianity as little more than Judaism for the Gentiles. When treating the martyrs themselves, Frend begins by announcing his concern to demystify their stories and more especially to expose the "pious romance" of late–nineteenth-century French Catholic historians who accepted the historical accuracy of the early martyr accounts at face value. For Frend, the task of the historian is to discern what kernel of truth, if any, might lie beneath the "stereotyped and florid discourses" that grew up around the martyrs. With access to a greater range of histori-

49. Robin Darling Young, *In Procession Before the World: Martyrdom as Public Liturgy in Early Christianity* (Milwaukee: Marquette University Press, 2001), 2.

50. W. H. C. Frend, *Martyrdom and Persecutions in the Early Church: A Study of a Conflict from the Maccabees to Donatus* (Garden City, NY: Doubleday, 1967), 55.

cal documents and the physical evidence of archeology, the modern historian stands poised to break through to the reality lying beyond the distorting haze of literary form.[51]

Frend's brand of rationalism remains dominant within the historical profession, yet recent developments in postmodern theory have opened up some space for less dismissive interpretations. Drawing in part on Clifford Geertz's narrative understanding of culture as "a story we tell ourselves about ourselves," some recent historians have focused on the meaning expressed in the texts of early martyrdom apart from the issue of the historical accuracy of those texts.[52] Elizabeth A. Castelli's *Martyrdom and Memory: Early Christian Culture Making* stands as a representative work of this new history. Castelli begins her study with a personal anecdote from her childhood Confirmation class. She notes that for all of the doctrinal instruction involved in the preparation for the sacrament, she and her classmates focused most of their attention on the choice of a Confirmation name—the name of the saint she was to take as a model for her adult spiritual life. Castelli identifies this ancient practice as an act of "communal history," a participation "in a ritualized practice of collective memory."[53] She then attempts to provide a sympathetic account of how the texts of early martyrdom initiated this tradition of culture-making through promoting identification with the great heroes of the faith. Castelli rightly argues against those historians who, influenced by Michel Foucault's history of private life, have tried to shoehorn the martyr narratives into the meta-narrative of the rise of interiority. Conceding "the context of a . . . public, collective narrative," Castelli nonetheless understands the individual martyr narratives as crafted and structured "to draw attention to the *production* of the martyr's self."[54] That the martyr

---

51. Frend, x–xii, 99.

52. For this understanding of culture, see Clifford Geertz, "Deep Play: Notes on the Balinese Cockfight," in his *The Interpretation of Cultures* (New York: Basic Books, 1973): 412–53.

53. Elizabeth A. Castelli, *Martyrdom and Memory: Early Christian Culture Making* (New York: Columbia University Press, 2004), 2.

54. Castelli, 70. Emphasis added.

models himself on the crucified Christ appears almost incidental to the meaning of the martyr narratives. An advance of sorts over Frend's rational skepticism, Castelli's approach stalls at a kind of textual agnosticism that privileges the process of cultural production over the substance of the culture produced.

Frend and Castelli stand as representative examples of the rival versions of moral enquiry that Alasdair MacIntyre has identified as encyclopedia and genealogy.[55] A third rival, which MacIntyre calls tradition, has yet to make its presence felt in the historical profession. This fact should come as no surprise, since, as we will show later, the historical profession took shape as a deliberate, self-conscious rejection of anything that might appear to be a traditional approach to history—that is, an approach in which the subject matter studied could properly serve as an authoritative, normative guide to study itself. In seeking to recover a traditional approach to history, we do not intend to reject the insights of encyclopedia and genealogy. We should be aware of the factual limitations of the accounts of early martyrdom; we should also be aware of the various narrative instabilities, lacunae, and aporias that present themselves in most of these texts. All this awareness need not diminish the authority of texts that continue to present enduring models of devotion to Christ and his Church. Not all martyr accounts are equally inspiring; some speak more directly to the concerns and challenges of our time than do others. Though all share the ideal of presenting a model for the imitation of Christ, they do so in different ways. If the redemptive sacrifice of Christ on the Cross is the doctrine that all Christians must accept, the retelling of that sacrifice through the stories of particular and idiosyncratic martyrdoms constitutes the culture that Christians need to foster in order to sustain and incarnate that timeless truth.

The classic martyr narrative is, of course, the account of the stoning of Stephen found in the seventh chapter of the Acts of the Apostles. Stephen's heroic defiance of the Sanhedrin has an enduring

---

55. Alasdair MacIntyre, *Three Rival Versions of Moral Enquiry: Encyclopaedia, Genealogy, and Tradition* (Notre Dame, IN: University of Notre Dame Press, 1990).

romantic appeal, reflected, for instance, in James Joyce's naming his fictional alter ego in his *Portrait of the Artist as a Young Man*. Stephen stood alone before his accusers and died beholding a vision of Jesus, yet his martyrdom was in no way the solitary act of a lone righteous man. The Acts of the Apostles is the story of the birth of the Church, not a collection of stories about holy individuals. Stephen's death demonstrates the truth that Tertullian would later capture in his famous dictum, "The blood of the martyrs is the seed of the Church." Some martyr narratives such as *Letter of the Smyrnaeans* (the martyrdom of Polycarp) focus on individuals, while others, such as the *Acts of the Scillitan Martyrs*, focus on groups. In no account, however, does the martyr give witness as an isolated individual. The *Letter of the Smyrnaeans* tells of Polycarp's Christ-like endurance of suffering: "for Polycarp, just like the Lord, had patiently awaited the hour of his betrayal—in token that we too, taking our pattern from him, might think of others before ourselves. This is surely the sign of a true and steadfast love, when a man is not bent on saving himself alone, but his brethren as well."[56] To approach the texts of martyrdom from within a Catholic historical tradition, we need first to look to those aspects of our living tradition that today stand most in need of renewal through engagement with the past. In a time when Catholics left, right, and center all too readily understand faith as primarily an individual commitment, the Catholic historian should labor to recover this communal corrective.

For understanding the communal dimension of martyrdom, few accounts surpass *The Passion of Saints Perpetua and Felicity*. Martyred at Carthage in the year 203 under the persecution initiated by Septimius Severus, Perpetua and Felicity quickly rose to the highest rank of the martyr saints of North Africa. Some two hundred years later, North African Christians held the passion narrative of these saints in such esteem that St. Augustine himself had to warn his flock not to put it on the same level of Revelation with sacred Scripture. No mere

---

56. "The Martyrdom of Polycarp," in Andrew Louth, ed., *Early Christian Writings* (New York: Penguin, 1987), 125.

regional saints, Perpetua and Felicity found a place in the Roman Canon; priests today continue to proclaim their names in the prayers that accompany the celebration of the Eucharist at Catholic churches throughout the world. Sadly, like so many of the early martyrs, Perpetua and Felicity survive as little more than names, overshadowed by the sheer volume of saints canonized since their time, as well as by the changing standards of sainthood deemed most relevant to contemporary spirituality. Parents seeking to inspire a life of good works in their children would understandably steer clear of *The Passion of Saints Perpetua and Felicity*. The narrative offers no edifying spirituality of everyday life; rather, it presents authentic Christian witness as in many ways a rejection of the best that everyday life has to offer, that is the duties, joys, and filial love of family life.[57] Although some feminist historians try to read modern notions of autonomy into accounts of early Christian female martyrdom, Perpetua and Felicity's passion narrative shows two women abandoning their natural families only to embrace the supernatural family of the Church. In an age that all too easily conflates Christian faith with natural "family values," this is a timely story indeed.

Those who think the problematic nature of the study of the past a dilemma of recent vintage should take heart from the opening chapter of the *Passion*. The prologue to the passion account begins by simultaneously praising the power of writing to preserve memory, and lamenting the burden memory of past greatness places on present action:

> If ancient examples of faith kept, both testifying the grace of God and working the edification of man, have to this end been set out in writing, that by their reading as though by the again showing of the deeds, God may be glorified and man strengthened; why should not new witnesses also be so set forth which likewise serve either end? Yea, for these things also shall at some time be ancient and necessary to our sons, though in their own

---

57. Caselli notes the lack of the routine details of everyday life characteristic of contemporary Stoic texts of self-fashioning. Caselli, 85.

present time (through some reverence of antiquity presumed) they are made of but slight account.[58]

At first glance this appears a rather contentious beginning for a presumably simple, pious text. The hint of generational chauvinism, if not conflict, reflects certain tensions within both classical and Christian understandings of the meaning of the past. Greco-Roman culture of the early Christian period invested the past with great authority and often dismissed Christianity as a novelty due to its relatively recent origins. Christians countered by claiming Jewish antiquity as their own and investing the Apostolic Age with a special authority binding on all subsequent generations of Christians.

Christians nevertheless conceded that the Apostolic Age was a novelty of sorts—it was something new and unprecedented, a heroic age of preaching the Good *News* of Jesus Christ, an historically unique, unprecedented person who made all things new. Inverting the conventional preference for the old over the new, Christians retained the Old Testament of the Jews while preaching the superiority of the New Testament of Jesus Christ. Thus, the author defends this contemporary story by reminding his readers that "those things which are later sought for their very lateness be thought the more eminent, according to the abundance of grace appointed for the last periods of time" (22).

Still, we should not confuse rhetorical sparring with generational revolt. The author of the prologue seeks ultimately to raise the present on par with the past, so "that no weakness or failing of faith may presume that among those of old time only was the grace of divinity present" (23). He writes not to celebrate "the prophecies and the new visions" for their own sake, but "of necessity both [to] write them and by reading celebrate them to the glory of God" (22, 23). This story of the present will soon be a story of the past, but the passion narrative will transcend time as Christ transcends time. The author writes so

---

58. Perpetua, *The Passion of SS. Perpetua and Felicity MM. A New Edition and Translation of the Latin Text Together with the Sermons of S. Augustine Upon These Saints,* trans. W. H. Shewring (London: Sheed and Ward, 1931), 22. All subsequent citations to this text will be parenthetical following the quotation or paraphrase.

"that both ye who were present may call to mind the glory of the Lord, and ye who now know by hearing may have communion with those holy martyrs, and through them with the Lord Jesus Christ, to Whom is glory and honor for ever and ever" (23).

A modern reader might find this prologue something of a bait and switch. The next section of the passion, a first-hand account written by Perpetua herself (the earliest surviving writing by a Christian woman), has surprisingly little to say about Jesus Christ. Even as Perpetua prepares for—and longs for—the ultimate imitation of Christ through martyrdom, the drama of the account focuses on her struggle against her natural family and desire to maintain communion with her new, supernatural family, her fellow martyrs. Perpetua's account begins by placing herself in a family context: she is both daughter and mother. A Christian catechumen under a house arrest of sorts, Perpetua rebuffs the efforts of her father to make her abjure her faith. Her father is angry with her and threatens her with physical violence. She concedes that he "strove to hurt my faith because of his love," yet sees his entreaties as "arguments of the devil." She rejoices when her father departs "vanquished;" she then receives baptism and is sent to prison along with her infant son and several Christian companions (24).

Perpetua's relation to her family is complex and ambiguous. Even as she presents her father as a devil, she receives comfort from her mother and brother. She is "tormented" by care for her son and gives him over to her family, yet suffers from his absence; when her family returns her son to her care, "the prison was made a palace for me" (25). Clearly Perpetua does not take these natural ties lightly. Still, the first half of her account builds up to the dramatic public break with her family duties as daughter and mother. On hearing of her impending trial, Perpetua's father makes one last appeal to her to renounce her faith:

> Have pity, daughter, on my grey hairs; have pity on thy father, if I am worthy to be called father by you; if with these hands I have brought thee unto this flower of youth—and I have preferred you before all thy brothers; give me not over to the reproach

> of men. Look upon thy brothers; look upon thy mother and mother's sister; look upon thy son, who will not endure to live after thee. Forbear thy resolution; destroy us not all together; for none of us will speak openly against men again if thou sufferest aught (27).

Perpetua's father may be a devil, but he is a devil with a heart; the devil is perhaps never more seductive than when tempting the faith with a lesser good so intimately bound up with authentic duty and love. Her father continues to abase himself before her, "fatherwise in his love, kissing my hands and grovelling at my feet," addressing her "not daughter, but lady." This is all for naught. Perpetua refuses to renounce her faith, and her father departs "very sorrowful" (27). Her father makes one last plea, as Perpetua and her companions stand public trial before Hilarian the procurator. Holding her son, he pleads with her "Sacrifice; have mercy on the child." She refuses, responding simply, "I am a Christian" (28). Condemned to the beasts, she awaits execution, troubled by the fate of her infant son. Denied access to him by her father and fearing he will die for lack of her nursing, Perpetua learns that he has begun to take solid food. She interprets this development as the will of God, "that I might not be tormented by care for the child and by the pain of my breasts" (28). Perpetua thus faces her martyrdom free from all of her family obligations.

These profoundly moving exchanges between Perpetua and her family speak powerfully to the challenge Jesus sets before his disciples with respect to family life (Mt 10:35–37):

> I have not come to bring peace, but a sword. For I have come to set a man against his father, and a daughter against her mother, and a daughter-in-law against her mother-in-law; and a man's foes will be those of his own household. He who loves father or mother more than me is not worthy of me; and he who loves son or daughter more than me is not worthy of me.[59]

---

59. Biblical quotations are taken from *The Bible, Revised Standard Version, 2nd Catholic Edition* (San Francisco: Ignatius Press, 2006).

Still, Perpetua does not understand her impending martyrdom simply in terms of her personal commitment to Jesus. Interspersed throughout her narrative, Perpetua recounts several visions relating to her passion. Whereas the proto-martyr Stephen saw a clear vision of Jesus Christ right before his death, Perpetua's visions focus on her companions. In her first vision, she ascends a bronze ladder to heaven. Studded with swords, spears, hooks, and knives, the ladder symbolizes the passion she will have to endure. As she nears the top of the ladder, she meets her companion Saturus, who had suffered martyrdom while Perpetua remained in prison. He greets her by name: "Perpetua, I await thee." Only after seeing her companion does she encounter "a man sitting, white-headed, in shepherd's clothing," who greets her by type: "Welcome, child." This Christ-figure stands as her final destination, yet he remains an allegorical figure, somewhat distant and remote in comparison with Saturus (26). Similarly, her final passion vision begins with her encountering the spirit of another martyr, Pomponius the deacon. Clothed in a white robe, he leads her into the amphitheater, saying: "Perpetua, we await thee; come." At the threshold of the arena, Pomponius performs the role of Christ, saying, "Be not afraid; I am here with thee and labour together with thee" (31).

Accounts by Saturus and about Felicity comprise the second half of the narrative and reinforce the communal themes of Perpetua's account. In Saturus's vision, Perpetua accompanies him to heaven, where they meet their departed companions Jocundus, Saturninus, Artaxius, and Quintus. Saturus and Perpetua immediately inquire about the rest of their companions, only to have angels interrupt and remind them to "Come first, go in, and salute the Lord" (33). After an encounter with another obscure Christ figure—"a man, white-headed, having hair like snow; youthful in countenance"—the vision concludes with a vision of the communion of saints: "we began to know many brothers there, martyrs also. And we were all sustained there with a savour inexpressible which satisfied us" (34, 35). The portrait of Felicity returns to the family themes of Perpetua's account, stressing perhaps even more forcefully the abandonment of family for the Church. Felicity is pregnant as she awaits her execution at the games. She suffers less from concern for her child than from fear that her condition will exempt her from suffering martyrdom with her companions, leaving her to "shed her holy and innocent blood after the rest, among strangers and malefactors" (35). Though still in her eighth month, she and her companions pray for an early labor. God answers their prayers: "she was delivered of a daughter, whom a sister reared up to be her own daughter" (36). The account then abruptly turns to the events leading up to the day of martyrdom in the arena. We hear no more of Felicity's daughter, beyond Felicity "rejoicing that she had borne a child in safety, that she might fight with the beasts . . . from blood to blood, from the midwife the gladiator, to wash after her travail in a second baptism" (38).

True to the intentions stated in the prologue, *The Passion of Saints Perpetua and Felicity* both celebrates the communion of saints in its narrative and sustains that communion through the retelling of the story over subsequent centuries. St. Augustine, who cautioned against excessive reverence for the narrative, nonetheless read it and preached on it every year on the feast day of the martyrs. A severe critic of the popular amusements of pagan Roman society, Augustine saw in the sacrifice of martyrs in the arena an alternative Christian spectacle, an inversion of pagan values in which the weak triumph over the strong: "Every year loving-kindness watches in a religious service what ungodliness committed on one day in an act of sacrilege."[60] Indeed, the stories of the martyrs provided the foundation for a broader Christian culture that spread through preaching, art, and the various liturgical celebrations that structured the everyday life of Christians for the next fifteen hundred years.


IT IS A COMMONPLACE to observe that Christianity is an historical religion, a system of beliefs, practices, and institutions that bases its claims upon unique events in the past. The role of narrative in sus-

---

60. Augustine quoted in Castelli, 124, 125.

taining Christian communities is thus a subject upon which further reflection seems both appropriate and timely. Prior to the rise of the modern historical profession, Christians not only cultivated the field that is their own past history, but were careful to hone and to keep free from rust those tools necessary for that cultivation. In mystery plays and Christmas carols, in stories told along pilgrimage routes and in letters sent back to Europe by far-flung missionaries, in sermons on saints and in accounts of the deaths of the martyrs, and, most especially, in the annual commemoration of the saving acts of God: in all these ways and others still, Christians throughout the centuries have made the business of remembering, rejoicing about, and giving thanks for the deeds of their ancestors and the Providential mercy of God the central expression of their faith. And they will continue to do so, whether professionals calling themselves historians choose to join them in that task or not. As practitioners of the historian's craft, it is our conviction that the tools we employ can be best employed within and at the service of the Christian tradition and, moreover, that Christian communities stand to gain from the historian's craft rightly employed.

# CHAPTER ONE

# *Catholicism and "That Noble Dream"*

TO BE A CHRISTIAN is to be bound by the past. Most of the sacred texts of the Old and New Testaments deal with historical events, and the ultimate truth of Christianity depends on the historical reality of the Incarnation of Jesus Christ in a particular place at a particular time. The New Testament gives us not simply the life and teaching of Jesus and their interpretation by St. Paul, but the Acts of the Apostles, a history of the first generation of the Church. The lifting of the Roman persecutions in the early fourth century inspired not simply thanks and praise, but an historical reflection on those persecutions, Eusebius' *Ecclesiastical History of the Church*. When the dream of a Christian Roman empire seemed to collapse in the early fifth century, the great Church father St. Augustine wrote *The City of God* to explain the collapse as not simply a consequence of human sinfulness, but an episode in God's providential plan of history. History, unlike most of the modern disciplines of the social sciences, has firm roots in the Catholic intellectual tradition. Catholics have been writing history of one kind or another for as long as there have been Catholics. The answer to the question, "What is a Catholic approach to history?" seems simple: continue to do what other Catholics have done before.

That answer actually held up fairly well until quite recently. The rise of distinctly modern approaches to the study of the past have, however, increasingly cast doubts upon the viability of that answer. Founded in 1884, the American Historical Association has struggled to define the discipline of history as something more than literature but less than science; however, it has consistently and unambiguously rejected any kind of confessional history as incompatible with the theoretical middle ground of common-sense empiricism that shapes conventional professional practice.[1] The renewal of Catholic historiography must begin with a proper understanding of the cautionary tale of the Church's engagement with modern secular historical thinking. Catholic history may indeed benefit from the more rigorous models of empirical verification bequeathed by modern secular history, but history will be Catholic only to the degree to which historians understand these facts within one of the various interpretive frameworks offered by the Church. The continuing authority of nineteenth-century conceptions of "objectivity" remains the single greatest intellectual impediment to the revival of distinctly Catholic interpretive traditions. A brief look at the fraught history of historical "objectivity" suggests the ways in which the opposition between reason and tradition now looks more like a battle between rival traditions—with objectivity a kind of existential bad faith incapable of meeting its own truth standards of correspondence and coherence.

---

1. For the most complete overview of the development of historical thinking and writing in its modern professional context, see Peter Novick, *That Noble Dream: The "Objectivity Question" and the American Historical Profession* (Cambridge: Cambridge University Press, 1998). For an earlier study, see John Higham, *History: Professional Scholarship in America* (Baltimore: Johns Hopkins University Press, 1965). For the broader institutional and cultural context for academic history, see Laurence R. Veysey, *The Emergence of the American University* (Chicago: University of Chicago Press, 1965) and Burton J. Bledstein, *The Culture of Professionalism: The Middle Class and the Development of Higher Education in America* (New York: Norton, 1976). On the relation between these developments and religious higher education, see George M. Marsden, *The Soul of the American University: From Protestant Establishment to Established Nonbelief* (New York: Oxford University Press, 1994) and Philip Gleason, *Contending With Modernity: Catholic Higher Education in the Twentieth Century* (New York: Oxford University Press, 1995).

## History, Objectivity, and Narrative

By nearly all accounts, the course of modern historical practice turns on the intellectual career of one man: Leopold von Ranke (1795–1886). It is Ranke, more than any other single figure, whom historians credit with the development of scientific, professional history writing.[2] When the emerging class of professional historians in America founded the American Historical Association in 1884, they named Ranke an honorary member, proclaiming him "oldest and most distinguished living exponent" of scientific history, indeed the father of historical science.[3] The scientific character of Ranke's history lay in his emphasis on bracketing the "opinions" of all previous historians and investigating an historical problem by drawing on primary, archival sources. The scientific historian would, moreover, examine "critically" as many sources as possible with an eye to conflicting and contradictory accounts of a single event. Scientific historical reason would adjudicate these conflicting accounts based on the evidence alone, free from the biases of received traditions.

This is the story that professional historians told themselves about their patron saint and founder. The real story of Leopold von Ranke is more complicated. Ranke's ideal of history has a history rooted in the political struggles of the nineteenth century. Ranke spent most of his professional life at the University of Berlin. A relative late comer in the world of German universities, the University of Berlin was founded in 1810 in the wake of the disastrous defeat of the Prussian army by Napoleon in 1806 and 1807. The Prussians interpreted this humiliating loss as a symptom of a deeper cultural backwardness in

---

2. For an overview of Ranke and the German historical tradition, see Georg Iggers, *The German Conception of History: The National Tradition of Historical Thought from Herder to the Present* (Middletown, CT: Wesleyan University Press, 1983). For an old, but still respected, biography of Ranke, see Theodore H. Von Laue, *Leopold von Ranke: The Formative Years* (Princeton, NJ: Princeton University Press, 1950).

3  David M. Darlington, "Distinctions for Distant Scholars: The AHA and Honorary Foreign Members," *Perspectives on History* (February 2009), accessed via internet, http://www.historians.org/perspectives/issues/2009/0902/0902tim1.cfm; Novick, 26.

the face of the modernizing forces of the French Revolution. Despite their own significant historical contribution to the rise of state bureaucracies, Prussian leaders saw in the revolution the creation of an even more integrated and efficient state bureaucracy. The University of Berlin was to be an institution for building up a Prussian version of this new model state through the training of citizens and civil servants to staff a growing state bureaucracy.

This new model of political organization demanded a new model of knowledge. Whereas universities of old served the common good by passing on a shared intellectual heritage, the new university would serve the public by emphasizing the development of new knowledge through original scientific research—knowledge that would empower the nation-state in its struggle with rival, modernizing states. History would empower the state by participating in the general promotion of the scientific ideal and the more specific legitimation of the nation-state system through historical research. Ranke earned his position at the University of Berlin in 1825 largely due to his *Geschichte der romanischen und germanischen Völker von 1494 bis 1514* (*History of the Romanic and Germanic Peoples from 1494 to 1514*), in which he traced the emergence of the modern state and balance of power politics back to the wars of early modern northern Italy. In going directly to the sources, Ranke may have left behind previous interpretations, but he brought with him a clear political teleology.

Ranke also brought with him a theology, or at least a philosophy. Nationalism shaped the work of all the historians of the nineteenth century, but Ranke's German nationalism carried with it a uniquely German philosophical idealism. As Peter Novick has pointed out, American historians completely missed this aspect of Ranke's thought in claiming him as their founding father.[4] Ranke's reputation as a cold-blooded scientific empiricist stems largely from a misunderstanding of a passage from the introduction to his book on the wars of early modern Italy, in which he defined objectivity as "not the duty to judge the past, nor to instruct one's contemporaries with an eye to the future,

4. Novick, 28.

but rather merely to show *how it actually was* [*wie es eigentlich gewesen*]."[5] American historians interpreted this last phrase as a commitment to empirical verifiability, whereas Ranke understood actuality more in terms of philosophical essence, a truth that transcends mere empirical data.

Ranke was a Hegelian as well as an empirical historian, and in many ways saw empirical rigor as simply putting the meat on the bones of a Hegelian historical teleology. He was also a Lutheran, and included God in his understanding of history. In linking history to philosophy and God, Ranke once wrote: "While the philosopher, viewing history from his vantage point, seeks infinity merely in progression, development, and totality, history recognizes something infinite in every existence: in every condition, in every being, something eternal, coming from God."[6] Again, no less a secular authority than Peter Novick has emphasized that Ranke's religious sensibility was no mere sentimental afterthought in his study of history. In a revealing passage, Ranke once wrote:

> God dwells, lives and can be known in all of history. . . . Every deed attests to Him, every moment preaches His name, but most of all, it seems to me, the connectedness of history in the large. It [the connectedness] stands there like a holy hieroglyph. . . . May we, for our part, decipher this holy hieroglyph! Even so do we serve God. Even so we are priests. Even so we are teachers.[7]

An exalted view of the historian's vocation to be sure, but one that carries with it a corresponding humility and sense of accountability in the face of a responsibility to an authority far greater than the standard of empirical accuracy.

---

5. Iggers, 67.
6. Leopold von Ranke, "On the Relations of History and Philosophy," in Georg G. Iggers and Konrad von Moltke eds., *The Theory and Practice of History* by Leopold von Ranke, trans. Wilma A. Iggers and Konrad von Moltke (Indianapolis and New York: Bobbs-Merrill, 1973), 38.
7. Quoted in Novick, 27.

## Narrative Nationalism and the
## American Historical Profession

American historians had no use for such religious language. The historical profession in America established itself as part of a larger social-scientific revolt against religious authority and asserted the autonomy of science with respect to all external authorities, be they religious, political, regional or institutional.[8] Despite their insistence on specialization and greater empirical rigor, the first generation of professional historians, men like Frederick Jackson Turner, Charles Beard, and Vernon Louis Parrington, looked down on the previous generation more for a lack of detachment than a lack of details. They dismissed George Bancroft's sweeping *History of the United States* because it offered a history of Andrew Jackson from the perspective of a Jacksonian Democrat, thus reducing history to political propaganda at best, or autobiography at worst.[9] The new historians committed themselves to the ideal of writing history free from such personal and political biases. They understood historical inquiry as the pursuit of empirically verifiable facts about the past and the establishment of verifiable relations of cause and effect among these facts.

If the first generation of professional historians left behind God and philosophy, they too, like Ranke, brought with them a teleology at once epistemological and political, one in which history would

---

8. On this development, see in general Mary O. Furner, *Advocacy and Objectivity: A Crisis in the Professionalization of American Social Science, 1865–1905* (Lexington, KY: University of Kentucky Press, 1975); Thomas Haskell, *The Emergence of Professional Social Science: The American Social Science Association and the Nineteenth-Century Crisis of Authority* (Urbana, IL: University of Illinois Press, 1977); and Dorothy Ross, *The Origins of American Social Science* (Cambridge: Cambridge University Press, 1991). These works are in many ways merely an institutional history gloss on the classic intellectual history of this period, Morton Gabriel White, *Social Thought in America: The Revolt Against Formalism* (New York: Viking Press, 1949). For a very different view of these developments that reflects the general argument advanced in this book, see Christopher Shannon, *Conspicuous Criticism: Tradition, the Individual and Culture in American Social Thought, From Veblen to Mills* (Baltimore: Johns Hopkins University Press, 1996).

9. Novick, 46.

demonstrate the complementary rise of critical reason and American freedom. For the link between politics and history, we need look no further than the name given to the first historiographical school to emerge from the new professional institutional setting of history writing. "Progressive" marks an era of both American politics and American history writing, dating roughly from the early 1890s to the early 1940s. Progressive politicians saw government as a tool for promoting democracy by restraining the power of capitalist corporations. Progressive historians saw history as a struggle between "the people" and "the interests." Taking the side of the people, they generally endorsed the Progressive politics of their time as an authentic embodiment of the spirit of popular democracy. The leading practitioners of Progressive history—Turner, Beard, Parrington, and Carl Becker—all drew inspiration from Germanic academic rigor, yet all directed that rigor toward telling a very American story of American history, in which America emerged as the last best hope for freedom in the world.[10]

That American nationalist history expressed itself differently than its contemporary European equivalents reflects both institutional and cultural differences between Europe and America. Unlike Germany, for example, the United States had no integrated national university system. Many of the leading research universities were private institutions, and the public university system arose under the political control of the states, as opposed to the federal government. This relatively decentralized institutional structure lent itself to a peculiarly American kind of regional nationalism. The first great Progressive historian, Frederick Jackson Turner, was a man of the Midwest who spent most of his professional career at the University of Wisconsin. Turner's fa-

---

10. The classic work on the Progressive historians remains Richard Hofstadter, *The Progressive Historians: Turner, Beard, Parrington* (New York: Knopf, 1968). See also Cushing Strout, *The Pragmatic Revolt in American History* (New Haven, CT: Yale University Press, 1958); Lee Benson, *Turner and Beard: American Historical Writings Reconsidered* (Glencoe, IL: The Free Press, 1960). For more recent studies, see Ernst Breisach, *American Progressive History: An Experiment in Modernization* (Chicago: University of Chicago Press, 1993) and David S. Brown, *Beyond the Frontier: The Midwestern Voice in American Historical Writing* (Chicago: University of Chicago Press, 2009).

mous "frontier thesis"—the argument that American democracy grew out of the primordial experience of pioneers encountering untamed nature on the Western frontier—challenged not only the "germ theory" that explained democracy as the fruit of political structures that first took root in the primeval forests of Germany, but also the received American wisdom that democracy sprung full grown out of the genius of the Founding Fathers of New England and Virginia. Still, in challenging orthodoxy and received tradition, Turner simply wished to claim American democracy for his own region.

Turner's privileging of the unsettled West against the civilized East reflects a deeper, broader anti-institutionalism that has shaped American culture since the nation's founding break with England. Turner's challenge to East Coast civilization was mild compared with that of his most notable successor within the school of Progressive history. Charles Beard burst on the scene in 1913 with his provocatively titled monograph, *An Economic Interpretation of the Constitution.* In Beard's work, the spirit of scientific materialism shifted its focus from the environment to economic interests.[11] Through extensive research in primary documents relating to the delegates at the Constitutional Convention, Beard concluded that the Founding Fathers structured the Constitution in such a way as to serve their economic interests. Though like Turner a Midwesterner, Beard's irreverence toward the East Coast establishment had broader nationalist implications. Beard traded Turner's dialectic of civilization and savagery for one of "the people" versus "the interests," a narrative with greater potential to unite Americans across regions in a contemporary struggle against "the interests" of his own time, the Robber Barons who plundered and oppressed the suffering masses of industrial America. Beard's irreverence towards elites was matched only by his reverence for the people, thus fostering a uniquely American nationalism at odds with most of its European contemporaries.

---

11. For book-length studies of Beard, see Ellen Nore, *Charles A. Beard: An Intellectual Biography* (Carbondale, IL: Southern Illinois University Press, 1983) and Clyde W. Barrow, *More Than a Historian: The Political and Economic Thought of Charles A. Beard* (New Brunswick, NJ: Transaction Publishers, 2000).

Beard's narrative was far more politically contentious than Turner's. His work elicited shock and outrage among the general reading public, leading many of his colleagues within the profession to question his commitment to scholarly detachment and objectivity. Beard, at the very least an honest man, questioned this commitment more searchingly than any of his contemporaries. Rejecting the charge that he had reduced history to political propaganda, Beard nonetheless could not bring himself to accept the image of detached, neutral objectivity enshrined in the founding of the American Historical Association. Although increasingly at odds with the profession, he became one its most visible and public figures and remained enough in the professional fold to earn election to the presidency of the American Historical Association in 1933.

## Faith and History in a Secular Key

Beard took this honor as an occasion to reflect on his own relation to the problem of objectivity. In his presidential address, "Written History as an Act of Faith," he rejected the understanding of history "dominant among the schoolmen during the latter part of the nineteenth century and the opening years of the twentieth century— the conception that it is possible to describe the past as it actually was, somewhat as the engineer describes a single machine."[12] Against this naïve scientism, Beard insisted on the inescapably subjective or personal element of history flowing from the preconceptions of the historian. Historians do not simply present facts, they select certain facts from a broad range of existing facts. This selection is an act of choice on the part of the historian and "any written history inevitably reflects the thought of the author in his time and cultural setting."[13] Insisting on this subjective dimension to the study of the past and drawing on the thought of Benedetto Croce, Beard under-

---

12. Charles A. Beard, "Written History as an Act of Faith," *American Historical Review* 39, no. 2 (January 1934): 221.

13. Ibid.

stood history as thought about "past actuality" rather than past actuality itself.

Acknowledgment of this inescapably subjective element in the study of the past need, however, entail no abandoning of the empirical or scientific method. Beard rejected relativism as facile and self-contradictory. Despite its limitations, "objective" history marked a tremendous advance in our knowledge of the past. Empiricism was, moreover, "a value in itself—a value high in the hierarchy of values indispensable to the life of a democracy." The passing of simplistic notions of objectivity "means no abandonment of the tireless inquiry into objective realities." Instead, it demands simply that we extend our inquiry into subjective realities as well. Faced with the reality of subjectivism, the historian must "examine his own frame of reference, clarify it, enlarge it by acquiring knowledge of greater areas of thought and events, and give it consistency of structure by a deliberate conjecture respecting the nature or direction of the vast movements of ideas and interests called world history." Beard closes on a prophetic note: "The historian may seek to escape these issues by silence or by a confession of avoidance or he may face them boldly, aware of the intellectual and moral perils inherent in any decision—in his act of faith."[14]

For a twenty–first-century Catholic looking back on the emerging profession of university-based history from the outside, Beard's position appears nothing short of reverent. At the time, it struck secular professional insiders as nothing short of blasphemy.[15] Beard raised the issue of belief in the title of his presidential address and continued to invoke religious analogies in responding to his professional critics. In submitting his formal response to the *American Historical Review*, his classic essay "That Noble Dream," Beard attached a note expressing his confidence that "our good old Church (AHA) is broad enough to include true believers and heretics."[16] Beard's response failed to per-

---

14. Ibid., 227, 229.

15. Novick, 268.

16. Ibid. Novick makes much of the religious language employed by these mostly secular Protestant men of the early twentieth century. He judges that "the hor-

suade his critics, who continued to denounce him as a traitor. Though the AHA did prove a Church broad enough to retain Beard as a member, Beard had long shifted the focus of his writing away from narrowly professional concerns in search of a broader audience. Beard's popular writings reveal the stakes of modern history writing to be much higher than the issue of objectivity. His historian's "faith" extended far beyond his responsible relativism to the propagation of a particular, though hardly unique, vision of man and society.

Much like his contemporary rebel historian Carl Becker, Beard envisioned the vocation of historian finding its fulfillment in public history of the very best sort—one that combined the empirical rigor of the new professional history with the narrative depth of a primitive, tribal bard.[17] The modern bard, however, sings not of the past but of history. He presents not timeless, universal models of excellence that reveal essential truths about human nature, but rather tells stories of change over time, of the constant trans-valuation of values. Historical accounts of Beard's populism and politics too often focus on his advocacy of progressive reforms or his later critique of Franklin Roosevelt's foreign policy.[18] Beard's politics went to the root, and for secular historians, the root is man. No vulgar propagandist, Beard was a sophisticated and subtle propagator of a vision of man and society designed to transcend the time-bound particulars of Progressive reform.

---

ror of relativism resembled the common horror of atheism." With the passing of denominational tests for service in public office in the early nineteenth century, local and state governments still demanded that public servants affirm their belief in God. At the time, such a belief generally implied a belief in hell, and those who set the rules of politics believed that the threat of eternal damnation would serve to keep public officials honest. For Novick, historians of the early twentieth century simply could not see how one could trust any scholar "not inhibited by an objectivist superego." See Novick, 269–70.

17. See, for example, Carl Becker, "Everyman His Own Historian," *American Historical Review* 37, no. 2 (January 1932): 221–36. For biographical studies of Becker, see Charlotte Watkins Smith, *Carl Becker* (Ithaca, NY: Cornell University Press, 1956) and Burleigh Taylor Wilkins, *Carl Becker: A Biographical Study in American Intellectual History* (Cambridge, MA: M.I.T. Press, 1961).

18. See, for example, Hofstadter's treatment of Beard in his *Progressive Historians*.

We see a classic rendering of this vision in the "Introduction" to Beard's most enduring work, his sweeping narrative history *The Rise of American Civilization* (1930). A popular work, it still bears the mark of the profession. If anything, Beard turned from the profession to the people only to more widely disseminate the worldview developed within the profession. Students of Progressive history will be surprised to find in his vision very little of the classic trope of the conflict between "the people" and "the interests." Beard's language is anthropological rather than political. In stating as his goal the presentation of American civilization as a whole way of life, cutting across the spheres of politics, economics, social life, and culture, he anticipates the vogue of Boasian cultural anthropology that would dominate intellectual life in the later 1930s; at the same time, his insistence that this organic whole is constantly changing and developing reflects his continued indebtedness to the nineteenth-century language of evolutionary biology. Beard's anthropological approach operates within the categories of base/superstructure distinctions common to nineteenth-century materialists (most notably Karl Marx), yet he reverses the conventional normative ordering: for Beard, material reality provides a base to foster and nourish a vibrant culture, but culture provides the privileged standard by which to judge any civilization. No more than Ranke is Beard willing to confine history to the spade work of empirical reconstruction. History requires vision. Whereas Ranke looked to Hegelian idealism, Beard drew on the tropes of reform Darwinism and American Pragmatism, defining the history of a people as "the philosophy of the whole social organism in process of becoming." No passive witness, the historian may be an active participant in this process, for the "history of a civilization, if intelligently conceived, may be an instrument of civilization."[19]

Beard's unprofessional tone obscures a deeper consensus on values shared with his critics in the American Historical Association. The most uncompromising Victorian defender of scientific objectivity in

---

19. Charles A. Beard and Mary R. Beard, *The Rise of American Civilization* (New York: The MacMillan Company, 1930), ix, vii.

history nonetheless believed that the professional, scientific study of the past somehow contributed to the betterment of society. Nor would Beard's professional colleagues object to his fundamental understanding of betterment: the advancement of human freedom understood as freedom from external constraint. A passage from the opening paragraph best captures Beard's sense of how an understanding of organic unity and dynamic growth all ultimately serve the cause of advancing human freedom:

> Dealing with all the manifestations of the inner powers of a people, as well as the trappings of war and politics, the history of a civilization is essentially dynamic, suggesting capacities yet unexplored and hinting of emancipation from outward necessities. By the sharp questions it raises in every quarter it may give new direction to self-criticism and creative energy, aid in generating a richer "intellectual climate," and help in establishing the sovereignty of high plan, design, or ideal.[20]

For Beard, history is process. Man studies the past in order to understand how this process works so as to better control it in the service of human freedom. Beard understands this freedom as primarily cultural rather than economic. His study of the economic motives of the Founding Fathers forever earned him the label of a quasi-Marxist materialist and critic of capitalism, yet the moral animus of his "Introduction" lies in his effort to bring business and culture together into a more fruitful union.

Beard devotes a surprising amount of space to articulating the vocation of the historian as facilitator of this union in the service of artistic patronage. In this capacity, the historian serves as tutor to both the businessman and the artist. The historian instructs the man of business that modern trade and industry cannot thrive in an intellectual and artistic desert.

---

20. Ibid., vii.

> Business enterprise has been built upon a heritage of civiliza-
> tion, and its directors are likely to be civilized just in proportion
> as they understand the history of their heritage without which
> they would be as economic infants.... They are in their turn the
> makers of civilization as well as patrons of the arts. In some mys-
> terious way thought and the materials of life evolve together.[21]

At the same time, artists must realize that the greatest art has
grown out of an engagement with a social and economic reality beyond
the rarefied world of the artist: "Take feudalism out of Scott, Victorian
poverty out of Dickens, modern urban misery out of Zola, and what
would be left? Or at all events, what would be the significance of the
vestiges?"[22] Historians will save artists from the temptation of art for
art's sake by reminding them of the inseparability of the artist from a
social milieu, and then explaining that milieu to the artists:

> We cannot escape the conclusion that with changes in civili-
> zation come changes in the nutriment which feeds writers and
> moralists, and in the materials with which they work. Then it
> follows that an ideal history of a civilization would help to ex-
> plain writers to themselves, audiences to audiences, actors to
> actors while disclosing the reciprocal relations of writers, au-
> diences, and actors. The profounder, wider and more realistic
> the history, the greater its services presumably to letters and
> criticism.[23]

The union of artistically minded businessmen and socially aware
artists is essential to the development of civilization. By what standard
do we judge development? How do we know we are achieving civilization? To answer this question, Beard—the hard-boiled economic
materialist—invokes no less a Victorian aesthete than Walter Pater.
A great age depends upon great artists, "personalities, many-sided

---

21. Ibid., xi.

22. Ibid., ix.

23. Ibid., ix–x.

and concentrated," or in Beard's words, "complex and complete personalities." Artistic "genius" depends upon originality, which in turn depends upon the artist's engagement with the dynamic, changing, developing civilization around him. The artist-as-historian stands as the ideal citizen of a properly developing civilization; the Beardian historian, in turn, becomes something of an artist.[24] The reader of Beard, by participating imaginatively in this dialectic, also becomes something of an artist.

Beard is far from the first writer to invoke the Romantic artist as the ideal modern person. The Romantic artist as privileged personality survived well into the Victorian period and became a stable of sentimental literature. No less a "conservative" figure than Lyman Beecher claimed Byron as his favorite poet. That Beard concludes his "Introduction" by invoking Voltaire as a model for his history writing suggests the deeper roots of his critical sensibility. It was this sensibility—that is, the common sense of Enlightenment modernity—that kept Beard within the fold of professional academic history despite his skepticism regarding the objectivity question. Enlightenment modernity is that broad Church within which the AHA is simply a local parish. The faith of the historian rests in a vision of man and society, not an epistemology, in capitalist material development and Romantic spiritual development, not scientific objectivity. If some more antiquarian professionals disdained Beard as a popularizer, they could take comfort in knowing that Beard was popularizing the worldview of the professional class. That enough of the general public responded favorably to Beard to make him the voice of history for a generation suggests the degree to which an Enlightenment narrative of progress had become a kind of common sense for the reading public of America.

## The Return of Liberal Reason

Fundamental agreement on the basic narrative of history enabled a certain tolerance on more abstract matters of epistemology. As that

---

24. Ibid., viii.

narrative came under attack with the rise of totalitarian regimes in the 1930s, Beard's type of relativism came to seem more and more like treason. Debate raged within the intellectual classes as to whether fascist and communist philosophies of power were the consequence of a post-Enlightenment relativism or a return to a pre-Enlightenment authoritarianism.[25] With the outbreak of World War II, politics trumped intellectual debate. In search of a certitude capable of underwriting a fighting faith, Western intellectuals circled the wagons around a liberal vision of Enlightenment modernity that had no place for Beard's style of relativism.[26] Liberal freedom and human rights were absolute values that transcended the contingencies of historical change.

Still, as World War turned to Cold War, liberal intellectuals struggled to find some way to take an absolute stand against Soviet communism without appearing absolutist. The historian Arthur Schlesinger Jr. imagined liberalism as a "vital center" between the extremes of totalitarian communism on the left and totalitarian fascism on the right.[27] For the two decades following World War II, liberal intellectuals spoke increasingly of a liberal "consensus" that united all Americans. The consensus consisted of a set of shared values and political commitments: in the area of culture, liberal Americans affirmed intellectual freedom and the freedom of religion as individual rights; on the thorny issue of the relation between politics and economics, postwar liberals affirmed a "mixed" economy, somewhere between the extremes of state planning and laissez-faire capitalism, as the best way to balance individual freedom and social responsibility. As golden mean or liberal muddle, vital center liberalism seemed to offer the best of both worlds: temperamentally, it resonated with the tropes of flux and fluidity that animated Beard's vision of history, yet politically it called for firm resolve in fighting totalitarianism, particularly Soviet communism.

---

25. For the classic account of these battles, see Edward A. Purcell Jr., *The Crisis of Democratic Theory: Scientific Naturalism and the Problem of Value* (Lexington, KY: University of Kentucky Press, 1973).

26. See Novick, Chapter 10, "The Defense of the West."

27. Arthur M. Schlesinger Jr., *The Vital Center: The Politics of Freedom* (New York: De Capo Press, 1988).

In this Cold War context, epistemological arguments about the nature of historical knowing gave way to the need to revamp at least one aspect of the fundamental narrative undergirding professional historical writing. A new generation of historians rejected the old Progressive trope of the "people" versus the "interests"—not only for its affinity with Marxism, but for its simplicity. Richard Hofstadter, the greatest of these revisionist historians, chided the Progressives not for relativism, but for a kind of absolutism. Hofstadter interpreted the Progressive emphasis on conflict in American history as less a defect in scholarship than a symptom of psychological immaturity, a quest for black-and-white certainty in a world that actually offered no easy answers.[28] He dismissed the Progressives as latter-day Manicheans who tried to flee the complexity of history by taking refuge in a simplistic historical dualism. Hofstadter and his fellow revisionists accepted the reality of conflict in American history, yet denied that this conflict was simple, dualistic, or ideological. Economic interests have divided Americans at certain points in American history, but so too have regional, ethnic, religious, and political interests. The range of possible conflicting interests was so broad as to inhibit the formation of any single, master battle line of conflict. Still, Hofstadter saw more to American history than the drift of countless small-scale battles. These micro-battles found their common ground in a set of shared values—a consensus on the liberal values of individual freedom, religious and cultural toleration, and the mixed economy. Once again, history followed politics. Once again, the unifying force was not epistemology, but narrative. Once again, liberal historians presented their narrative as reality itself.

Revision breeds a new orthodoxy, which in turn breeds more revision. By the mid-1960s, liberal consensus historians found themselves under attack by a younger generation of radical, "New Left" historians. Drawing inspiration from western European Marxism and reaching back to homegrown American Progressivism, these New Left historians sought to re-center class conflict in American history

---

28. See in general Hofstadter, ibid.

and invest other sites of contention, particularly race and gender, with ideological significance. These historians accepted the historical reality of the liberal tradition in America to some degree, but tended to read American history as one long struggle against this liberal tradition. History was the story of "resistance" against liberalism, and it was the moral duty of historians to recover and recuperate the forgotten voices of the past suppressed by the triumph of liberalism.[29]

Interestingly, as bitter as the battle between liberal and radical historians became, both sides shared a rough consensus on the epistemological issues that had so shaken the first generation of professional historians. Each side accused the other of distorting the past for ideological purposes, but the accusation assumed a shared understanding of the past as a solid reality accessible through common-sense, empirical realism. The radicals proved even more epistemologically conservative, rejecting the consensus historians' emphasis on ideas and privileging the study of material, empirically verifiable reality. This hyper-empiricism stemmed in part from the logic of revision, in part from the development of statistical and quantitative methods in the social sciences, but undoubtedly also from the felt need to make some kind of irrefutable argument against their liberal detractors, many of whom remained in positions of professional power into the early 1970s.

## The Return of Liberal Faith

This generational struggle had the unintended consequence of forcing liberal historians to come clean on the values and the narrative that shaped their vision of history. In retrospect, it is hard to see "consensus" history as anything other than an overarching view of the past, but during its formative period, its practitioners insisted that they approached history free from such ideological constructs. Liberalism was the anti-ideology ideology, so to posit it as the vital center of American history came near to denying any center to American history at all.[30] Attacks by New Left historians deprived liberals of

---

29. On these developments, see chapters 13 and 14 in Novick, ibid.
30. Novick, 408.

the luxury of this comfortable irony and forced them to take a stand not unlike that taken by an earlier generation of liberal historians on the eve of World War II. In times of crisis, with the barbarians at the gate, liberal history transforms scholarly detachment itself into a kind of fighting faith.

Two works by leading historians published in the heat of the crises of the late 1960s show mainstream liberal history with its guard down. The first of these is J. H. Plumb's *Death of the Past*. Plumb was one of the leading British historians of his generation. Based on a series of lectures delivered at City College, New York in 1968, Plumb's book tells the heroic story of the triumph of objective, scientific history over mythic histories rooted in religious, ethnic, and national traditions. It is a story that could have been told in 1884 at the founding of the American Historical Association, but Plumb's retelling reflects the particular challenges of the late 1960s. From the perspective of moderate liberalism, the radical movements of the time appear as symptoms of a kind of religious revival. The extreme radical Left shares with the extreme traditionalist Right a common abandonment of reason and a willingness to distort history in the service of some ideological or mythic agenda. Against the forces of unreason, Plumb affirms empirical accuracy and theoretical rigor as the only legitimate goals for history writing.

Despite his praise for Olympian detachment, Plumb concludes his lectures by revealing the faith that motivates his reason. At the end of the day, history does have a holy purpose: "The past can be used to sanctify not authority nor [sic] morality but those qualities of the human mind which have raised us from the forest and swamp to the city, to build a qualified confidence in man's capacity to order his life and to stress the virtues of intellect, of rational behavior." History, after all is said and done, does indeed teach a truth:

> It is to me the one truth of history—that the condition of mankind has improved, materially alas more than morally, but nevertheless both have improved. Progress has come by fits and starts; retrogressions are common. Man's success has derived

from his application of reason, whether this has been to technical or to social questions. And it is the duty of the historian
to teach this, to proclaim it, to demonstrate it in order to give
humanity some confidence in a task that will still be cruel and
long—the resolution of the tensions and antipathies that exist
within the human species.[31]

That Plumb can describe the promotion of this all-encompassing
philosophy of history as a set of "limited objectives" merely reflects
the degree to which it was in his time the common-sense faith shared
by the vast majority of academic historians.

The second book of this moment, David Hackett Fischer's *Historians' Fallacies: Toward a Logic of Historical Thought*, stands as at once an
internal critique of this common sense and an affirmation of the fighting faith of historical reason. Written in 1970, it is a book in but not
quite of its time. Like Plumb, Fischer writes against the politicization
of history at the hands of radical scholars; unlike Plumb, he devotes
most of his book to unmasking the illusions that had sustained the
profession since its inception, subjecting common sense empiricism
to the most brutal beating one could imagine this side of Friedrich
Nietzsche. Any one making it through the three hundred pages of this
densely argued deconstruction of nearly every possible explanatory
framework at the disposal of professional historians might well wonder why anyone—most of all Fischer himself—would bother trying to
write academic history at all.

At the end of it all, however, Fischer concludes with what we can
only interpret as an affirmation of his faith in historical reason. The
alternative to existing historical fallacies lies in greater empirical and
theoretical rigor. Why should we bother with any of this? The pressing political needs of the day demand it:

The vital purpose of refining and extending a logic of historical thought is not merely some pristine goal of scholarly perfec-

---

31. J. H. Plumb, *The Death of the Past* (Boston: Houghton Mifflin Company, 1971), 141,
142.

tion. It involves the issue of survival. Let us make no mistake about priorities. If men continue to make the historical error of conceptualizing the problems of nuclear war in prenuclear terms, there will not be a postnuclear world. If people persist in the historical error of applying yesterday's programs to today's problems, we may suddenly run short of tomorrow's possibilities.[32]

Faced with the threat of nuclear annihilation, the duty of the historian "consists in teaching men somehow to think reasonably about their condition. Reason is indeed a pathetically frail weapon in the face of such a threat. But it is the only weapon we have."[33] Fischer's liberal *cri du coeur* is the type of existential affirmation that would continue to underlie most academic history even after "tenured radicals" had gained the power to define mainstream history.[34]

As radical students became radical professors, historical thinking experienced a period of relative epistemological calm. Populist politics actually reinforced epistemological conservatism. Turning from intellectual to social history, radical scholars of the 1970s and 1980s relied on common-sense empiricism to prove the historical reality of oppression and resistance. Despite its roots in conservative economic theory, cliometrics, or the application of statistical and quantitative models to the study of the past, provided a kind of gold standard for accuracy among empirically oriented historians. Of course, the turn to numbers provided no definitive account of the past; it simply shifted the terms of debate about the past toward numbers. In one famous instance, the conservative economists Robert Fogel and Stanley Engerman used cliometric models to empirically reconstruct the material life of African American slaves in the antebellum South. Their book, *Time on the Cross: The Economics of American Negro Slavery*, notoriously ar-

---

32. David Hackett Fischer, *Historians' Fallacies: Toward a Logic of Historical Thought* (New York: Harper and Row, 1970), 317.

33. Ibid., 318.

34. On the rise to power of sixties' radicals in higher education, see Roger Kimball, *Tenured Radicals: How Politics Has Corrupted Our Higher Education* (New York: Harper and Row, 1990).

gued that in material terms, the everyday life of slaves was not so different from that of the average white farmer in the Old South.[35] Left/liberal historians were outraged and accused Fogel and Engerman of excusing or defending the practice of slavery itself. Still, the official scholarly response met Fogel and Engerman on their own terms. In his *Slavery and the Numbers Game*, the radical labor historian Herbert Gutman argued that Fogel and Engerman had simply got their numbers wrong and that a more rigorous reading of the empirical data revealed that slavery was indeed a more materially immiserating experience than that of free white labor in the rural South.[36] This issue, indeed the whole field of social history, generated much heated and passionate disagreement, but all contained within a consensus on common-sense empiricism underwritten by an implicit faith in progress through reason much like that extolled by Plumb and Fischer.

This consensus chugged along productively through the 1970s and 1980s, incorporating an ever-wider range of previously marginalized groups into its big-tent view of history. The professional journals augmented the hot-button issues of class and race with articles on gender and sexuality, and, as we write, gay and lesbian history stands at the cutting edge of the profession. The price of admission for all these new subfields is assent to the above-described consensus. The social historians who presided over this widening of "the circle of we" soon found themselves in a dilemma.[37] These new groups often brought with them methodologies developed in other disciplines that challenged the common sense empiricism on which the historical profession relied as the guarantor of civil, rational discourse. In particular, understandings of the nature of the relationship between

---

35. Robert William Fogel and Stanley L. Engerman, *Time on the Cross: The Economics of American Negro Slavery* (Boston: Little, Brown, 1974).

36. Herbert G. Gutman, *Slavery and the Numbers Game: A Critique of Time on the Cross* (Urbana, IL: University of Illinois Press, 1975).

37. This phrase invokes David Hollinger's generally sanguine reading of the increasing ethnic diversity of the intellectual classes in postwar America. See among other works his David A. Hollinger, "How Wide the Circle of the We? American Intellectuals and the Problem of Ethnos Since World War II," *American Historical Review* 98 (1993): 317–37.

language and reality drawn from the various disciplines of literature and linguistics raised doubts about the ability of historians to reconstruct the past through empirical, archival research. This so-called "linguistic turn" questioned the very categories through which historians studied the past.[38]

Conventional historians recognized all sorts of "contexts" that shaped, enabled, and constrained the actions of past historical actors. Yet the linguistic turn raised the issue: how can we talk about social structure when the very category of class is historically contingent? If we move beyond a simplistic Marxist understanding of class as a position in relation to the means of production, then we only move into some other category that will inevitably produce some new blindness to accompany its new insight. What conventional historians understood as the refinement and progress of analytical tools, partisans of the linguistic turn were likely to see as the imposition of presentist categories on the past. The novelty of an analytic category became the best argument against its usefulness in understanding the past in its own terms. The dilemma of the historian, moreover, simply reflected the dilemma of the historical actors they studied. The vision of historical actors tossed about by contingent categories not of their own making threatened the whole concept of historical agency that had provided social history with its *raison d'être*. Using very differ-

---

38. The literature on the linguistic turn is vast. For the purposes of professional historical thinking, the best introduction may be found in a series of essays published in the American Historical Review in the late 1980s. See John E. Toews, "Intellectual History After the Linguistic Turn: The Autonomy of Meaning and the Irreducibility of Experience," *American Historical Review* 92, no. 4 (October 1987): 879–907; David Harlan, "Intellectual History and the Return of Literature," *American Historical Review* 94, no. 3 (June 1989): 581–609; David A. Hollinger, "The Return of the Prodigal: The Persistence of Historical Knowing," *American Historical Review* 94, no. 3 (June 1989): 610–21; David Harlan, "Reply to David Hollinger," *American Historical Review* 94, no. 3 (June 1989): 622–26; Allan Megill, "Recounting the Past: 'Description,' Explanation and Narrative in Historiography," *American Historical Review* 94 no. 3 (June 1989): 627–53; Joyce Appleby, "One Good Turn Deserves Another: Moving Beyond the Linguistic: A Response to David Harlan," *American Historical Review* 94, no. 5 (December 1989): 1326–332.

ent language, promoters of the linguistic turn channeled the spirits of Becker and Beard by arguing for the impossibility of that noble dream of objectivity.

The profession survived the assault of relativism redivivus and this time needed no common catastrophe such as World War II to bind the contending parties together. To be sure, the conservative turn in America politics during the Reagan era left many a left-liberal academic anxious to hold on to a secure center of institutional power; any full embrace of the linguistic turn would have been professional suicide. Still, intellectual inertia did much of the work needed to de-fang the linguistic wolf at the door. David Hollinger's statement of faithless faith in conventional practice spoke for the consensus of the profession:

> I do not know what ultimately explains our vocabularies and our practices, but I believe we must put at risk in research the theories we find most promising. I do not possess a calculus for measuring the relative agency of authorial intention, but I believe that authors remain present enough in texts to justify our listening for their voices. I do not understand the mystery of knowing, but I believe this mystery has survived the return of literature.[39]

The linguistic Left, in turn, seemed willing to reign in its more radical epistemological claims in the interests of professional peace and political progress. John Boswell, one of the pioneers in the field of gay history, recognized that the very term "gay" is anachronistic when applied to same-sex relations much before the nineteenth century; however, he also insisted that if contemporary gays were to create a history that would validate their humanity and affirm the dignity of their lifestyle, then they needed some trans-historical category around which to rally. By committing an act of intellectual bad faith, gays and lesbians would gain admission into the grand liberal historical narrative of liberation through reason.[40] And they did. Not all were

---

39. Hollinger, "Return of the Prodigal," 621.

40. John Boswell, "Concepts, Experience, and Sexuality," in Edward Stein, ed., *Forms*

willing to go quietly in the night, and minor skirmishes persisted into the early 2000s. Still, as recently as 2009, AHA president Gabrielle Spiegel announced yet another death of the linguistic turn and proclaimed the dawn of yet another "new era of historical concerns."[41] More work needs to be done, and an army of professional historians stands ready to be up and doing.

Thus stands the American historical profession in the early twenty-first century. For all of the intellectual challenges of the twentieth century, the average professional historian remains a spiritual brother to a Victorian rationalist such as Frederick Jackson Turner. This spiritual brotherhood is anathema to authentic Catholic history, for it requires submission to the god of Enlightenment reason and an historical narrative that sets the freedom of the individual against the authority of all received traditions. The Catholic encounter with this new professional practice began as a sincere effort at inculturation, an attempt to mine Egyptian gold from a discipline in so many ways hostile to the Church. In the American context, the Catholic intellectual missionaries went native, so to speak, ultimately forcing Catholic intellectual traditions to conform to secular norms. The renewal of Catholic historiography depends upon a proper inculturation of the achievements of modern professional history. To set us on the proper path, we must first understand the wrong road we have traveled.

## Popes, Archives, and Objectivity

By one reading, the Catholic intellectual tradition offers few points of intersection with the account of the historical profession we have just rendered. Digging in its heels against modernity and revolution, the Church simply stood on the sidelines as the rise of historical consciousness progressed through the nineteenth century. Bishop Gaspard Mermillod of Geneva declared that the proclamation of papal

---

*of Desire: Sexual Orientation and the Social Constructionist Controversy* (New York: Routledge, 1992).

41. Gabrielle M. Spiegel, "The Task of the Historian," *American Historical Review* 114 (February 2009): 3.

infallibility at Vatican I "set the nations free from history."[42] Against history the Church upheld tradition, and affirmed the pope as the ultimate arbiter of the meaning of tradition. Pius IX declared, "I am the Tradition," and his successor Leo XIII called for a renewal of the study of the thought of St. Thomas Aquinas in order to combat the growing influence of historical-critical approaches to the Bible within the Catholic theological movement known as Modernism. Thomism dominated Catholic intellectual life until the Second Vatican Council and presented itself as a defender of timeless truth against all the varieties of philosophical relativism that flourished in mainstream secular thought during the twentieth century. Liberal Catholics often figured their revolt against Thomism and the whole culture of pre–Vatican II Catholicism as the fruit of the discovery of historical consciousness. In his *Bare Ruined Choirs*, for example, Garry Wills traced his liberation from Catholic tradition to the discovery of *"the dirty little secret . . . that the Church changes."*[43]

This story of the Catholic flight from history is only half true. In his 1879 encyclical *Aeterni Patris*, Leo XIII did indeed call for a revival of Thomism precisely because of its perceived ahistoricity; however, four years later the same pope wrote his "Letter to the Three Cardinals," in which he formally opened the Vatican archives to scholars and declared that the Church had nothing to fear from historical studies.[44] Leo's actions were the fruit of an almost century-long struggle with the emerging discipline of professional history. Even as secular nationalists achieved the increasing marginalization of the Church in political life, they craved access to Vatican documents to reconstruct their own national histories defined in large part through the struggle to achieve independence from the papacy.[45] Leo was convinced that a

---

42. Quoted in James Hennesey, S.J., "Church History and the Theologians," *U.S. Catholic Historian* 6, no. 1 (Winter 1987): 2.

43. Garry Wills, *Bare Ruined Choirs: Doubt, Prophecy, and Radical Religion* (Garden City, NY: Doubleday, 1972), 21.

44. Owen Chadwick, *Catholicism and History: The Opening of the Vatican Archives* (Cambridge: Cambridge University Press, 1978), 100.

45. Ibid., 22.

fair reading of the documents held at the Vatican Archives would prove the Church no necessary enemy of legitimate national aspirations. He was also convinced that only a thorough scholarly treatment of the history of the popes could defend the office of the papacy against the harsh, negative treatment it had received at the hands of non-Catholic historians, not the least being Leopold von Ranke himself.

The full story of the opening of the Vatican Archives is long and complicated. For the purposes of this essay, we will focus on the papacy's relation to the development of historical studies in Germany that would so shape the American historical profession. Owen Chadwick, the critical yet somewhat sympathetic historian of the opening of the archives, places the Vatican at the scene of one of the earliest turning points "in the history of the discovery of truth in history."[46] In 1821, the German scholar G. H. Pertz requested and gained access to documents pertaining to the pontificate of Pope Honorius III, a key figure in the long struggle between the papacy and the German emperor Frederick II. At the time, no archive allowed free and open access to its collections. That the Vatican allowed an outsider (Pertz was Protestant) of no particular scholarly reputation access to sensitive documents purely in the interests of scholarship was, if not unprecedented, certainly exceptional for the time. The decision reflected both a respect for German scholarship among certain Vatican officials and a sense among the Curia that the Church might be able to exert some influence on the intellectual life of Europe were it to build up Rome as a center of scholarship.[47] Still, the Vatican proceeded with caution. For most of the next sixty years, it provided access to documents relevant to national histories through copies made upon request by individual scholars. During this period, no unauthorized Catholic could enter the archive under pain of excommunication.

Through the middle of the nineteenth century, popes continued to vacillate back and forth on access to the archives and the issue of history in general. Often papal decisions reflected a particular pope's

---

46. Ibid., 23.
47. Ibid.

relative sense of security with respect to the very real threats of secular nationalists (the declaration of papal infallibility took place as Italian nationalist troops invaded Rome and annexed the Papal State into the new nation of Italy). The excommunication of the controversial Catholic historian Johann von Döllinger by Archbishop von Scherr in 1871 no doubt reflected a defensive posture in response to Bismarck's *Kulturkampf.* The turning point in Leo's thinking came in 1883. Once again a German Protestant scholar played a key role in the Church's thinking about archival history. Pietro Balan, the sub-archivist at the archive, allowed Theodor Sickel, a German Protestant scholar, access to the *Privilegium Ottonis,* a document on which the papacy based its claims to lands in central Italy yet which Protestants had long denounced as a forgery. Sickel was one such Protestant; nonetheless, after examining the document, he declared it to be authentic. This, for Leo, showed that the Church could meet critics on their own terms, and emerge victorious.[48] In 1884, a year after officially opening the archives to scholars, Leo addressed a group of German Catholic historians and urged them, "Go to the sources. That is why I have opened the archives to you. We are not afraid of publishing documents out of them."[49]

Happy to have Protestant scholars confirm the historical claims of the Church, Leo nonetheless wished to see Catholic scholars take the initiative to write grand sweeping histories that could pass empirical muster with the new scientific scholarship, yet remain faithful to the Church's understanding of its past. In this, Leo set his sights as high as possible, hoping to take on the work of the leading scientific scholar of the age, Leopold von Ranke. Historians tend to emphasize Ranke's technical and methodological principles, yet his reputation during his lifetime rested on his subject matter as much as his method. Ranke earned his reputation for objectivity most decisively through the publication of his multi-volume *History of the Popes* (1834–39). Compared to previous historians, Ranke seemed to have raised the history of the

---

48. Ibid., 99.
49. Ibid., 103.

papacy above the polemics of the Reformation. Still, for most Catholic readers, Ranke's history bore the imprint of his Lutheranism—not through direct falsification, but through tone, attitude, and selection of documents and topics.[50] Leo longed for a Catholic historian to champion the cause of the papacy. He found his historian in Ludwig von Pastor.

A German by birth and later an Austrian diplomat, Pastor first learned history under one of the leading Catholic historians of his day, Johann Janssen. It was his mentor Janssen who first inspired Pastor to write a Catholic alternative to Ranke's history of the papacy. Pastor came of age during Bismarck's *Kulturkampf.* Critical of Ranke's icy detachment, Pastor wrote as a soldier in a culture war; nonetheless, he embraced the new spirit of objectivity and rejected any reduction of Catholic history to apologetics. Pastor took advantage of the opening of the Vatican Archive and immersed himself in the sources. The first volume of his history appeared in 1886. It met with a cool reception by non-Catholic scholars. Based on exhaustive archival research, it still struck the wider scholarly community as a work of apologetics. It was not until the publication of the third volume in 1895 that Pastor finally earned respect outside of Catholic circles. This volume dealt with the Renaissance papacy and presented a frank and unflattering portrayal of the most notorious pope of the era, the Borgia Alexander VI. Pastor insisted that the sinfulness of individual popes actually proved the divine nature of the Church as an institution, but his willingness to expose papal sin to public scrutiny led some members of the Curia to call for the placing his book on the Index of Forbidden Books. Leo intervened on behalf of Pastor and praised his work as a model for a history at once Catholic and scientific.[51]

Leo held firm to his commitment to the study of Catholic history, whatever sins it might reveal. Addressing the issue of clerical education at the end of the decade, the great proponent of the Thomistic revival also insisted on the need for clergy to study and write honest

---

50. Ibid., 117.
51. Ibid., 116–27.

Catholic history. Echoing St. Augustine, Leo declared, "God does not want our lies." Catholic historians were "to keep back nothing of the trials which she [the Church] has had to experience in the course of the ages through the frailty of her children and sometimes even of her ministers."[52] For Leo as for Pastor, the scandals of Church history only confirmed the divine nature of the institution. No purely human institution could have survived such weakness.

At the turn of the century, few scholars outside of the Catholic world shared Leo's confidence in the arrival of a mature Catholic historical imagination. Despite conceding some honesty and bravery on the part of Pastor, non-Catholic scholars continued to dismiss Catholic history as a branch of Catholic apologetics. No amount of archival research could excuse the conclusions Catholic scholars drew from their study of the past—conclusions that affirmed the timeless truths of Thomistic philosophy and the very timely politics of ultramontanism.[53] Such criticisms are to some degree no doubt warranted, yet they assume an ideal of objectivity nowhere visible among secular historians of Pastor's time, or our own. That Ranke was a Hegelian in philosophy and a nationalist in politics has not diminished his standing in the history of history. We do not mean to defend Pastor against Ranke at a technical level; yet even the epigones of Ranke seem to merit standing as "real" historians, whereas the best of confessionally Catholic historians remain outside the brotherhood.

## Catholicism, Professionalism, and Americanism

We see this double standard at work even more so in the American Catholic context. General awareness of the master narratives that

---

52. Quoted in Thomas J. Shelley, "God Does Not Need Our Lies," *Commonweal* 122: 31 (April 7, 1995), 31.

53. Catholic scholars who fully embraced the professional model were all too willing to affirm this criticism. It has long been *de rigueur* for any Catholic historian looking back on the early efforts at professional Catholic history to dismiss ultramontanism as a relic of the confessional past. For one symptomatic example, see Eric Cochrane, "What Is Catholic Historiography?" *The Catholic Historical Review* LXI, no. 2 (April 1978): 169–90.

shaped Progressive history has in no way diminished the standing of the great Progressive historians such as Turner, Beard, and Becker. They remain the standard by which historians judge the work of American Catholic historians writing during the formative period of the historical profession. Catholic historians examining the work of John Gilmary Shea (1826–92) and Peter Guilday (1884–1947) have generally found them lacking in sufficient rigor and detachment. Shea, a layman, introduced the archival approach to Catholic history in America and founded the U.S. Catholic Historical Society in 1884. Though committed to objectivity and of an utterly unphilosophical bent of mind, he still wrote history that was faithful and deferential to the teachings of the Church. Guilday, a priest, co-founded *The Catholic Historical Review* in 1915 and The American Catholic Historical Association in 1919. According to the standard account, Guilday marks an advance in professionalism and objectivity, though he retained an attachment to some notion of God's providential activity. Subsequent generations would see further advance, culminating in the efforts of Guilday's greatest pupil, John Tracy Ellis (1905–92), to break all remaining links to apologetics and promote a thoroughly professionalized secular approach to history among Catholic historians.[54]

The struggle of Catholic historians to live up to the perceived higher standards of the American Historical Association was part of a larger struggle on the part of Catholic intellectuals to gain a hearing in American public life. The founding of the American Catholic Historical Association reflected in part the natural tendency of Catholics in the early twentieth century to form separate, distinct institutions that often paralleled institutional developments in the secular world.[55] It also reflected the real anti-Catholic prejudice that animated most

54. This narrative structures nearly every account of the development of Catholic historical thinking in America. For one representative example, see J. Douglas Thomas, "A Century of American Catholic History," *U.S. Catholic Historian* 6, no. 1 (Winter 1987): 25–49.

55. On this tendency, see Charles Morris, *American Catholic: The Saints and Sinners Who Built America's Most Powerful Church* (New York: Vintage Books, 1997), especially chapter 6, "A Separate Universe."

mainstream American institutions—especially educational institutions—in the first half of the twentieth century. Historians of American Catholicism were in a particularly difficult situation. Mainstream secular historians might very well have viewed the Catholic Church as the greatest force of evil in human history, but they conceded that it was impossible to study European history without dealing with the subject matter of the Catholic Church. Not so with American history. For most American historians, America was Protestant in its founding and despite increasing secularization remained fundamentally Protestant in its culture. Catholicism was a minority religion of immigrants that had no place in mainstream U.S. history. If American historians looked on Catholicism with contempt, many Catholic historians looked on America with contempt. For most Catholic historians, the real history of the Church lay in Europe; America was mission country whose history mattered only the degree to which it impacted events in Europe. Given this situation, we must understand Guilday and Ellis's promotion of objectivity as also a plea for broader cultural acceptance, indeed an effort at cultural assimilation.

Objectivity alone would not break down the barriers keeping Catholics outside mainstream intellectual circles. Only narrative could do that. The generations of historians guided by Shea and Guilday rarely challenged the ultramontane story of Pastor, yet to it they added a distinctly American story of the triumphant march of religious freedom. Catholic historians who look back with embarrassment on Shea's traditional Catholic theological orientation treat his celebration of the Catholic contribution to America as a prophetic, providential anticipation of the Vatican II document *Dignitatis Humanae*.[56] This theme has remained the guiding spirit of American Catholic history since Shea. It received official, mainstream recognition when the University of Chicago Press tapped John Tracy Ellis to write the volume on American Catholic history for its series on the History of American Civilization, edited by one of the leading "consensus" histo-

---

56. Again, see Thomas, ibid.

rians of the 1950s, Daniel Boorstin.[57] Ellis presented the history of the Catholic Church in America as primarily the story of the contribution of Catholics to American religious freedom. Ellis presents a respectful account of the struggles of generations of Catholics to pass on the faith across generations, but he ultimately subordinates this internal, religious story to the political story of the role of Catholics in contributing to the building of American civilization. *American Catholicism* is a consensus book for a consensus time, but also reflects an American Catholic narrative with deeper, broader roots in the nineteenth-century experience of an immigrant Church struggling to gain acceptance in the face of WASP, anti-Catholic nativism.

Ellis's influence extended far beyond the ranks of professional Catholic historians. It is safe to say that he is the single most significant figure in twentieth-century American Catholic intellectual life. At the same time as he was reaching out to a broader non-Catholic audience to reassure them of the commitment of American Catholics to religious pluralism, he was scolding his fellow Catholics for residual tribalism, parochialism, and general intellectual underachievement. This internal critique—really assault—reached its high (or low) point in Ellis's 1955 essay, "American Catholics and the Intellectual Life."[58] Ellis's essay has been the subject of countless articles and books.[59] For the purposes of this argument, we need only say that this essay set the agenda for American Catholic intellectual life for the next half century. It inspired two generations of Catholic educators to abandon distinctly Catholic intellectual traditions and hold Catholic educational institutions to the same standards as secular institutions. In 1967, Ellis's vision found its formal, institutional endorsement at the gathering of all the heads of American Catholic institutions of higher

---

57. John Tracy Ellis, *American Catholicism* (Chicago: University of Chicago Press, 1956).

58. John Tracy Ellis, "American Catholics and the Intellectual Life," *Thought* (Autumn 1955): 353–86.

59. For the best recent account, see John McGreevy, *Catholicism and American Freedom: A History* (New York: W. W. Norton and Company, 2003), especially chapter 6, "American Freedom and Catholic Power."

learning known as the Land O'Lakes Conference. University of Notre Dame president Theodore Hesburg led the call for the abandonment of Catholic identity, all the while insisting that this new openness to the world simply reflected the spirit of *aggiornamento* coming out of the Second Vatican Council.

It is no coincidence that an historian rang the alarm bell for Catholic intellectual life. Ellis lamented that secular schools such as Princeton and the University of Chicago were doing the best work in Thomistic philosophy, but he saw that the future of public intellectual life belonged to the social sciences. Though a few conservative Catholics still invoke natural law as a public philosophy, history has served American Catholic scholars as the primary language for engaging the non-Catholic world. This language has reflected both an epistemology of objectivity and a narrative of Americanism. Between the two, the commitment to America was older and never seriously questioned by any mainstream Catholic academic historian.

Like the non-Catholic academy, Catholic higher education found itself rocked by the liberal-radical civil war of the late 1960s. Unlike their non-Catholic counterparts, however, Catholic historians still felt the need to slay the dragons of confessionalism and affirm a commitment to objectivity. As late as 1971, John W. O'Malley, a Catholic priest who had earned the respect of the secular profession for his work in early modern European history, felt the need to draw once again a line in the sand between naturalism and providentialism: "God may have hardened Pharaoh's heart, but the historian is interested only in the contingent social, economic, and psychological factors which were at work on Pharaoh."[60] O'Malley's position was uncompromising: providentialism is for theologians, natural causality is for historians, and never the twain should meet in any properly academic setting.

O'Malley's gauntlet allowed for no middle ground. Our treatment

---

60. This passage comes from his essay "Reform, Historical Consciousness, and Vatican II's Aggiornamento," quoted in Philip Gleason, "History, Historical Consciousness, and Present-Mindedness," in Gleason's *Keeping the Faith: American Catholicism Past and Present* (Notre Dame, IN: University of Notre Dame Press, 1987), 207.

of modern history, both non-Catholic and Catholic, has suggested such a middle ground in narrative. Though most Catholic historians have been content to follow O'Malley's vision of natural/neutral causality, one historian of his time advanced a critique very much in keeping with our argument for the inescapability of some such middle ground. Philip Gleason, perhaps the most thoughtful participant-observer in these developments during the era of Vatican II, long ago argued that O'Malley had drawn his lines a bit too sharply. In his essay "History, Historical Consciousness, and Present-Mindedness," Gleason argued that O'Malley's position had the effect merely of exchanging one providentialism for another—that is, trading Catholic theology for secular philosophy. O'Malley's vision of a naturalist history free from theological distortion was shot through with tropes and assumptions drawn from the philosophical traditions that dominated the secular academy in the late 1960s. Gleason argued that when O'Malley spoke of "the discontinuity of the past" and the absence of "any overarching divine plan," or when he asserted that the "past is human ... to be understood in terms of man, who is free and contingent," he was simply speaking the language and invoking the framework of existential philosophy—that is, trading St. Augustine for Jean-Paul Sartre.[61]

Still, Gleason in no way meant to argue for the epistemological equivalency of Catholicism and existentialism. He registered his criticism of O'Malley as part of a larger critique of trends in post–Vatican II history writing that he felt compromised common sense empiricism in the service of some ulterior agenda, be it the secular philosophy that guided O'Malley or the radical politics that guided activist scholars such as David O'Brien. Gleason's alternative amounts to little more than an affirmation of what he admits to be a simple "common-sense realism." Abjuring extreme, absolutist standards of objectivity and neutrality, Gleason insisted that we can determine, within the limits of available empirical evidence, what actually did or did not happen in the past. Historians must be aware of those limits and open to revising their account in light of new evidence, but rational procedures exist

---

61. Ibid.

that can verify the reliability of such evidence as it appears.[62] Gleason's common-sense realism was not, however, narrative neutral. He wrote American Catholic history from within a moderate Americanist framework that affirmed the goodness and rightness of the American experiment with religious pluralism.[63]

A Catholic historian can, of course, in good conscience appeal to *Dignitatis Humanae* to affirm some aspects of America-style religious liberty. Still, religious liberty is at best instrumental to the more basic stories that sustain Catholic culture and evangelize the non-Catholic world. Gleason never directly rejected, ignored, or disparaged these stories, and he never adopted the stance of hostile autonomy that animated O'Malley's declaration of independence from Catholic tradition. The same cannot be said of most of Gleason's contemporaries and the subsequent generation of American Catholic historians trained by the Vatican II generation. This generation for the most part measured its intellectual autonomy by its degree of hostility to the authority of the institutional Church. In doing so, it accomplished nothing less than a revival of the old heresy of Americanism. As condemned by Leo XIII in *Testem Benevolentiae*, Americanism basically consisted in the presumption that the Church in America should conform itself to American political and cultural norms. As promoted by certain American churchmen in the late nineteenth century, Americanism went far beyond the affirmation of religious pluralism and toleration to argue for the democratization of Church institutional structures and the primacy of individual conscience in matters of moral and spiritual truth.[64] Americanism became the fighting faith of Vatican II–era liberal Catholic historians. They looked back to the early republic as

---

62. Gleason, ibid., especially the section "A Methodological Confession of Faith," 216–25.

63. Gleason remained committed to this vision throughout his career. On this, see Philip Gleason, "Becoming (and Being) a Catholic Historian, " in Nick Salvatore, ed., *Faith and the Historian: Catholic Perspectives* (Urbana, IL: University of Illinois Press, 2007): 7–30.

64. On Americanism, see Morris, chapter 5, "An American Church" and McGreevy, chapter 4, "The Nation."

a golden age for the Church, a lost moment of democratic lay authority that finally received Church approbation in the documents of the Second Vatican Council.

There is more than a little irony in how this Americanism functioned in the historical profession. Liberal Catholic historians saw it as their ticket to respectability and general professional acceptance. The secular profession as a whole was generally uninterested in the Americanizing Catholic Church, but instead was most attracted to the story of the world that the Americanizers wished to leave behind: the world of urban, ethnic, immigrant "ghetto" Catholicism. We see this irony in the career trajectories of the representative American Catholic historians of the two generations of scholars who have come of age since Vatican II, Jay P. Dolan and John McGreevy. Coming out of the 1960s, Dolan emerged as the first great Catholic hope. Educated at the University of Chicago Divinity School, Dolan joined the history department at the University of Notre Dame and achieved brief crossover stardom through his first book, *The Immigrant Church: New York's Irish and German Catholics, 1815–1865.*[65] Dolan rode the wave of social history that swept across the academy in the 1970s. With its empirical, archival rigor and use of sources that illuminated the lived experience of working-class urban ethnics, the book commanded the attention of secular scholars otherwise uninterested in Catholicism. Dolan presented his work as populist scholarship of a sort, a revolt against the old "brick-and-mortar" Catholic history that focused on priests and bishops who build the extensive infrastructure of the urban-ethnic Catholic ghetto. Still, Dolan's heart lay less with the immigrant masses than with the Anglophile, assimilationist, Americanized Church that greeted them upon their arrival. Sympathetic to immigrant hardship, Dolan was more than a little skeptical of immigrant faith, which tended to be far more traditional and deferential to authority than that of native American Catholics. Like so many secular social historians, Dolan valued traditions when they served as a basis

---

65. Jay P. Dolan, *The Immigrant Church: New York's Irish and German Catholics, 1815–1865* (Baltimore: The Johns Hopkins University Press, 1975).

for resistance to institutional authority, but rarely acknowledged them as a legitimate authority in their own terms.

Dolan's moment in the secular sun proved fleeting. Social history grew increasingly focused on race and gender issues, and Dolan's brand of liberal Americanism lagged far behind the political curve of the increasingly radical, New Left consensus that dominated the profession. Dolan's next book, *Catholic Revivalism*, focused on just those aspects of American Catholicism at the farthest remove from urban ethnicity, the itinerant religious preachers who promoted parish missions in the nineteenth century. Even if many of these missions were preached on ghetto Catholic terrain, Dolan chose to emphasize the similarities between Catholic mission preaching and evangelical Protestant revivalism.[66] Dolan's effort to chart the development of a distinctly American Catholicism reached its peak in his 1985 survey text, *The American Catholic Experience: A History from Colonial Times to Present*.[67] Here, Dolan produced what remains the standard Americanist account of American Catholic history. He framed this history with the following three-part structure: 1) an early national period (1789–1830) committed to forging a distinctly American style of Catholicism; 2) a traditionalist, immigrant phase (roughly 1830 to 1960) that rejected Americanism yet anticipated a later liberal Catholicism through its growing concern for social justice; and 3) a robustly liberal, Americanist phase (the period since Vatican II) that combined concern for social justice with a commitment to lay democracy within the Church. Liberal Catholic historians could celebrate this narrative as a moment of intellectual arrival, yet liberal Catholicism remained as much a ghetto in the profession as the old ultramontane Catholicism had been in an earlier period.

John T. McGreevy has filled Dolan's shoes for the current generation of scholars of American Catholicism. His career to date has followed a trajectory similar to Dolan's: a Catholic undergraduate degree

---

66. Jay P. Dolan, *Catholic Revivalism: The American Experience, 1830–1900* (Notre Dame, IN: University of Notre Dame Press, 1978).

67. Jay P. Dolan, *The American Catholic Experience: A History from Colonial Times to Present* (Garden City, NY: Doubleday, 1985).

(he was a student of Dolan's at the University of Notre Dame), followed by a secular graduate degree (he earned a Ph.D. from Stanford and a brief teaching appointment at Harvard) and a tenured teaching position at the University of Notre Dame. McGreevy earned his reputation largely due to his first book, *Parish Boundaries: The Catholic Encounter with Race in the Twentieth Century Urban North.*[68] The book was widely (and positively) reviewed in the scholarly and popular press. It places American Catholic history back on familiar ground, the ethnic urban ghetto. McGreevy takes Dolan's immigrant Church story into the twentieth century and looks at the persistence of an old ethnic tribalism during an era that Dolan characterized as dominated by liberal Americanism. In McGreevy's account, a tribalism once perhaps justified in the face of WASP nativism had, by the mid-twentieth century, degenerated into racism in its opposition to integrated housing.

McGreevy is certainly more sympathetic to the plight of Catholics than most historians of urban race relations. He concedes that Catholics were in many ways defending the integrity of their parish boundaries and local Catholic culture. Still, he holds them accountable for the sin of racism, a failure to join in the great American effort to right the historic wrongs of American slavery. There are good Catholic reasons to criticize the actions of urban Catholics on the front lines of racial integration. Popes throughout the twentieth century had condemned racism and American Catholic bishops generally supported efforts at racial integration during the Civil Rights era. Still, McGreevy judges his subjects less as bad Catholics than as bad Americans. That is, their failure lies less in their refusal to follow the Church's teaching and their clerical superiors than in their refusal to embrace the main currents of the American quest for social justice as represented by the Civil Rights Movement.

The Americanist trajectory of McGreevy's historical imagination is even clearer in his next work, *Catholicism and American Freedom*, a book universally praised by the Catholic historical establishment

---

68. John T. McGreevy, *Parish Boundaries: The Catholic Encounter with Race in the Twentieth-Century Urban North* (Chicago: University of Chicago Press, 1996).

in America.[69] Here we see McGreevy following the same path—and in many cases covering the same material—as his mentor Jay Dolan. Less a comprehensive survey than a monographic study of a single issue—as the title suggests, the relationship between Catholicism and American freedom—the book nonetheless reads like a subtle, nuanced updating of Dolan's *American Catholic Experience.* Once again, McGreevy shines on race, with an excellent chapter on Catholic attitudes toward slavery. Once again, he invokes Catholic communalism to temper the charge of racism: Catholics opposed emancipation not simply because of their negative attitude toward African Americans, but because of their suspicion of abolitionists who seemed to set themselves against every principle of social order that threatened to restrict individual freedom. This same communal ideal also inspired a deep suspicion of free-market capitalism and would later animate Catholic social teachings that McGreevy judges far in advance of liberal American thinking in the late nineteenth century. Finally, McGreevy takes anti-Catholic nativism as a serious force in liberal American politics and culture, not just the prejudice of backwoods bigots.

Still, for all his nuance and subtlety, ultimately McGreevy tells the story not of the tension between Catholicism and American freedom, but of the struggle of Catholicism to live up to the standards of American democracy. This becomes clear in the trajectory of the final three chapters of the book. After spending two chapters on "life" issues—that is, birth control, abortion, euthanasia, and biological engineering—McGreevy concludes his book with an account of the priest sex-abuse scandal. Ultimately, he judges it a symptom of the Church's inability to overcome its inherent (and un-American) authoritarianism. The scandal is less about sex than episcopal power, with the implication that it never would have happened if liberal Catholics had succeeded in democratizing the Church in the 1960s. We do not intend to minimize the enormity of clerical sex abuse, but surely American freedom itself has an even greater scandal in the fifty million abortions performed since the 1973 Supreme Court ruling of *Roe v. Wade.*

---

69. See the review symposium in *U.S. Catholic Historian* 21, no. 4 (Fall 2003): 87–106.

McGreevy's treatment of abortion is fairly balanced and sympathetic to the Catholic position, but like many a Catholic politician, McGreevy seems to think that his public professional life requires neutrality on Catholic issues even as it allows for heavy partisanship on secular issues. McGreevy's righteous anger at the clergy sex-abuse scandal follows the righteous anger he expressed on Catholic racism in *Parish Boundaries*. We have no objection to any historian taking a strong stand on these issues; we simply call attention to what appears to be a rather selective moral outrage, one attuned more to the priorities of American liberalism than to those of the Church.

## Faithless Histories

With McGreevy as with Dolan, Catholic historians pat themselves on the back and celebrate their arrival in the mainstream, while the profession yawns. American Catholic historians remain in a scholarly ghetto. Nearly all pursue their careers within historically Catholic institutions. They continue to write sweeping surveys that re-tell an Americanist story interesting mainly to an aging Vatican II-era liberal constituency.[70] Moreover, Catholics have forfeited their one opportunity to make a virtue of their provincialism. By the 1990s, the epistemological debates surrounding postmodernism spilled over into the field of American religious history. The Nietzschean perspectivalism that informed historians of race and gender seemed to give an opening to historians writing from religious traditions. In two books, *The Soul of the American University* and *The Outrageous Idea of Christian Scholarship*, the Reformed historian George Marsden retold the history of American higher education in a way that cast doubt on the standard progressive secular narrative and raised the possibility that Christian scholars might embrace the best of secular scholarship without bracketing their Christian traditions. Marsden's suggestion provided

---

70. See Jay Dolan, *In Search of American Catholicism: a History of Religion and Culture in Tension* (New York: Oxford University Press, 2002) and James M. O'Toole, *The Faithful: A History of Catholics in America* (Cambridge, MA: The Belknap Press of Harvard University Press, 2008).

the inspiration for years of conferences and publication projects generously funded by the Pew Charitable Trust and Lilly Endowment. Marsden advanced these views while a colleague of McGreevy's at Notre Dame, where he had the luxury of training up a new generation of Protestant scholars to implement his idea of Christian scholarship.

Marsden's idea of Christian scholarship is far from outrageous, but his use of the term presented a challenge to Notre Dame's understanding of its own commitment to Catholic scholarship.[71] On more than one occasion, McGreevy, as the leader in his field, was called upon to give the Catholic response to the Marsden thesis. McGreevy repeatedly re-affirmed the Land O'Lakes settlement. There is no distinctly Catholic scholarship. The professional disciplines are autonomous and to be judged by internal standards, which in history means reliance on facts and empirically verifiable causality. There is no more a Catholic history than a Catholic physics.[72]

This tired, slavish adherence to the fictional norms of objectivity remains the animating ethic of Catholic historians, whatever their field of study. This ethic of objectivity remains guided by either a narrowly Americanist or more broadly modernist historical narrative that holds history accountable to the ideal of progressive individual liberation through the advance of human reason. The possibility of a distinctly Catholic historical imagination appears only as a retreat from reason. In order to revive a distinctly Catholic historical imagination, we need to look back to a time before the separation of faith and reason, when Catholicism provided the foundation for a robust and imaginative engagement with every aspect of human life, including history.

---

71. For a critique of Marsden, see Christopher Shannon, "Between Outrage and Respectability: Taking Christian History Beyond the Logic of Modernization," *Fides et Historia* 34 (2002): 3–12.

72. John McGreevy, "Faith Histories," in Andrea Sterk, ed., *Religion, Scholarship, and Higher Education: Perspectives, Models, and Future Prospects* (Notre Dame, IN: University of Notre Dame Press, 2002), 63–75.

# CHAPTER TWO

# *The Historian's Craft and the Catholic Tradition*

IF WHAT WE HAVE observed about the practice of the professional historian be accurate, then the lot of the Catholic who wishes to practice the historian's craft seems to be particularly unfortunate. It is all well and good to admonish Christians to be in the world without being of the world. Yet the historian's craft is especially difficult to square with this principle. Society always needs soldiers, statesmen, and philosophers; these have a perennial social role that Christianity only deepens and directs. Yet the historian's craft is not one of ruling, but of making: the making of discourses, narratives, analyses, courses, lectures, museum collections, and monuments. His activity seems to be more like that of the cobbler, gardener, or haberdasher: deprive one of these tradesmen of the commonly accepted tools of his craft and he will no longer be making shoes, sowing seeds, or hemming suits, he will be out of work. Without the goal of the reconstruction of the past from sources and the autonomous community of historians mutually correcting one another in that pursuit, what sort of livelihood remains for the aspiring historian? The thought that there might be an alternative conception of the historian's craft, its tools, and its social role seems almost unthinkable. It is the task of this chapter to show that there is just such an alternative conception of the historian's craft, and that it is found by asking what role the historian may be called upon to play within the life of Christian communities and their search for the common good.

The goods held in common by Christian communities are in the first place spiritual. The life of a Christian and of a distinctly Christian community is to be characterized by the pursuit of the beatitudes, the gifts of the Holy Spirit, and the theological virtues of faith, hope, and charity. These spiritual goods are the fruits of the sacramental life of the Church, the personal prayer, sacrifices, and almsgiving of individual Christians, and also of the ordinary living of Christian callings in families, confraternities, religious communities, parishes, and other organs of the universal Church. The role of the historian's craft with respect to these spiritual goods is a dispositive one. Just as the craftsman working in a material medium provides some object that can be used in the course of the pursuit of those higher, spiritual ends, so also the historian and the poet, the philosopher, and even the theologian produce things made of words that help Christians to pursue their final end: the life of charity, both temporally and in eternity.

## Preliminary Objections

Even as we would begin to specify how the historian's craft may be understood to contribute to the life of charity, we are confronted with three significant objections to our attempt that come from different quarters of the tradition and community we wish to serve.

First is an objection to what seems to be an embrace of postmodern relativism on our part. The objection is that by discarding the master-narrative of the rise of liberal modernity as a triumph of reason, we have left reason with nothing to accomplish. If history cannot recount a verifiable and convincing narrative of human progress—so the objection may be expected to run—it has nothing left to do. The Church, moreover, has herself in recent years become the explicit defender of reason, as for instance in Benedict XVI's *Regensburg Address*, or in his warning in *Spe Salvi* against the kind of global critique of technology that would amount to a stance of ingratitude towards the gift of human reason. Surely, the objection continues, the rise of the professional or academic historian is itself an instance of the progress of reason, for it represents a healthy criticism of the follies, blindness, and sins of mankind. Just as repentance is the necessary precursor to faith, so historians, voluntarily self-limited to a critical use of reason, contribute to a kind of social repentance sorely needed in the modern world.

A second objection comes from philosophers and theologians, who remind us that history does not offer reliable insight into the works of God, nor even into the most pressing questions about man and society. For history, as such, is the record of particular events, and the knowledge of such particulars is merely an instrument for the sake of gaining knowledge of general truths and principles of timeless import. No quick rejoinder about the particularity of sacred history will serve to refute this objection, for the objection concerns the historian's craft as commonly understood, not as practiced by those few whose attention is given to the events disclosed in sacred Scripture and who, to the extent that they are attempting to shed light on the faith of the Church, may in fact be participating in the discipline of theology. No, this objection has in mind the craftsmen who study Greek medicine, Roman citizenship, medieval villages and communes, early modern martyrs and missionaries, patterns of immigration in the modern world, and countless other subjects besides. The force of the objection lies here: that the pursuit of knowledge about such matters is potentially limitless and, as such, intrinsically frustrating to the pursuit of wisdom, which is, in the last analysis, the knowledge of God as the first cause and final end of all things. History, on this account, encourages the vice of curiosity. No significant renewal of Catholic intellectual life, therefore, can be expected to follow from the labors of historians.

A third objection comes from our fellow historians. Your critique and proposal, they reasonably protest, cuts you adrift from the contemporary practice of history and leaves you companionless. You yourselves have affirmed that intellectual discourse serves a community, but you have no community. There is no educated public such as that sought by the Enlightenment; it has dissolved into the myriad self-referential sub-communities that populate the internet. All conversations are now irreducibly private, that is, when they rise to the level of conversation and are not merely monologues. There is, moreover, no identifiable Catholic intellectual community, for there is no discernible difference between the information-consumption of well-educated Catholics and that of their secular counterparts. And since the sophistication of your analysis leaves you speaking only to the well-educated, you really must address yourselves to the academy, for today the well-educated live only in the academy. But you seem to dismiss the academy by your analysis of the development of the historian's profession, and so you condemn yourselves to isolation. Your call for a tradition-based historical inquiry is, therefore, either hopelessly ambitious or self-refuting.

### Replies to Objections

In response to these objections, we frankly admit that not only are these the objections that have been made to us by respected colleagues, they are also the objections that confront us in our own reflections. Our global response to them is embodied in this essay as a whole. Yet to each of the discrete objections, an initial reply is in order.

To the first, we say that it is time to shelve narratives of progress. John Paul II showed us the way in *Evangelium Vitae*, which taught us to think of the story of modernity as a tragedy. Then there is the parable of the wheat and the tares, which hardly suggests any simple conception of human progress towards the Last Judgment. Nor does Christ's haunting question: "When the Son of Man returns, will he find faith upon the earth?" (Luke 18:8) As to the contention that the critical use of reason present in modern historiography can serve as a *praeambulum fidei*, we reply that any criticism of man or society is only as useful as the substantive account of authentic human flourishing upon which it is based. Just as there can be no satire without a high sense of man's dignity, so also there can be no critical history absent a compelling and accurate account of the common good. The common good rightly understood is the principle that historians are called upon to consider, and the exercise of right judgment using the common good as its measure is the virtue they are called upon to practice. By doing so, they can contribute to the good of the Christian communities they serve. It is from the perspective of understanding the common good as the shared life of virtuous activity—hardly a postmodern premise—that Enlightenment historiography appears the most impoverished. Our critique, therefore, frees reason to reclaim its proper role, the task of judgment.

To the objection of the philosophers and theologians, we reply first with gratitude; the subordinate art always stands to profit when careful attention is paid to it by the ruling or architectonic one. The greatest tragedy of Catholic intellectual life in our time is not, in fact, the straying of historians, but that of philosophers and theologians themselves. For, as Aquinas affirmed, it pertains to the wise man to rule, and especially to rule the things of the intellect. Although the vice of curiosity may be one to which historians are particularly prone, it is a vice that in a philosopher or a theologian is even more detrimental, because if those whose chief concern should be to refer all things to the end themselves fail to do so, how much more likely are they to stray whose studies carry their attention to things that are more remote from the end? Theologians and philosophers who think it a matter of indifference what cast of mind possesses their colleagues across the hall soon find themselves opposed in committees by historians, literary scholars, and other students of human culture who, having adopted some form of empiricism or postmodernism skepticism, cannot see any justification for their colleagues' fields. What is theology, a student of literature may well ask, other than literary criticism applied to a certain kind of text? And what is philosophy, wonders an historian, other than critical reason closing the door upon any claims to universal knowledge so that our empiricism can be embraced without second thoughts?

With philosophers and theologians, we affirm the real, if modest, ability of human reason, beginning with our common experience of the world, to attain some reliable knowledge of the natural world, human happiness, the common good, the immateriality of the soul, and the existence of God. To these, we ask: are we not likely to be much more reasonable exponents of the proper place of historical studies and narratives than our anti-philosophical colleagues? And we who affirm the high place of theological study and teaching, acknowledging it to be a science proceeding from the Revelation entrusted to the Church, and, consequently, affirming theology thus understood to be the rightful Queen of the sciences: if we are bold enough to insist upon the crucial though subordinate role of historical narratives in the renewal of Catholic intellectual life, will it not be reasonable to give our argument a hearing? To the second objection, then, our reply is that to be held accountable to a strong and persuasive vision of the pursuit of wisdom is precisely what historians most need.

And to the third, and in some ways most imposing objection, we reply that there are times when only the ventures of faith will suffice. We are convinced that the persons who most greatly suffer from the current state of the historical profession are Catholic historians themselves, constrained to lay bricks for Pharaoh when they wish to be singing in Zion. If we want our baker to take pride in a well-turned and nourishing loaf, then we must—Adam Smith notwithstanding—expect our bread from his benevolence, that is, from his firm intention to serve the common good with his craft and to deserve the recompense and the gratitude that is owed to good work faithfully done. In a similar way, if we want historians to be strengthened by a settled conviction that their craft is a noble one, we must restore the ordination of their craft to the common good rightly understood. There is no other solution. Whatever material or institutional price there is to be paid for such a restoration will have been well worth paying if the historian's craft produces a new generation of historians who, like Bede, Bossuet, and Newman, will instruct and delight many subsequent ages of students and readers.

## The Necessity of Judgment

It is precisely the ordination of the historian's craft to the final end of charity that must be considered. Just as the life of charity in the individual requires the mature practice of all the virtues, so also the common life of charity of a Christian community requires a mutual support, even mutual inculcation of the virtues, especially in the vital effort of the transmission of Christian culture. It is this effort of transmission, the task of education, where we find the historian's craft most properly located, for, as Alasdair MacIntyre has convincingly argued, it is in the various tasks associated with the transmission of the life of the virtues that the centrality of the virtue of right judgment becomes apparent.[1] This faculty of right judgment—a firm, habitual disposition to evaluate practical matters in light of an adequate conception of the common good—is, to be sure, a part of the larger virtue of prudence. Yet it can be isolated from the commanding of actions and thus be considered in its own right. It is, when so considered, the virtue the possession or absence of which makes one to be a good or a poor judge. And an historian is certainly some kind of judge, for what else would we call someone who weighs evidence about past deeds for the sake of delivering some account of them?

Yet to equate the historian and the judge immediately gives rise to another objection, the objection of the scientific historian, who flees judgment as necessarily distorting the past by the imposition of the judge's own vision and instead pretends either merely to the reconstruction of that past or, in some cases, to the determination of necessary relations of cause and effect that are brought under one or another law-like cause and thus rendered free of the taint of moral evaluation. On this view the historian is either a social scientist or a glorified archivist, and the product of his research is a value-neutral tool. Not only is this value-free history the proverbial pot of gold, as a candid inspection of the "noble dream" of twentieth-century historiography bears out, it is also the strangest of chimeras. Historians chronicle human things, but human things necessarily give rise to judgments about the good. The notion of a history devoid of the good is as self-refuting as a biology that denies the distinction between the living and the non-living: it is a discipline that has denied the existence of its only possible subject matter.

---

1.  See MacIntyre, *After Virtue: A Study in Moral Theory*, 2nd edition, 223.

Yet suppose that all of the counsels against judgment from Marc Bloch to Herbert Butterfield are practical advice and not statements of a theoretical first principle. Even here, however, we are left with a position that refutes itself. Their claim is that history is most truthfully practiced by historians who have no other end in view than the excellent practice of their art, from which principle it follows that the more self-referential the conversation among historians, the better it will be. And the more autonomous is that conversation, the more immune from external pressure from Church, State, or culture, the more free and pure will be its pursuit. This spectacle is a perplexing one: a group of artisans declare that their art exists purely for its own sake, with no further end in view beyond that of its own exercise and with no ties of dependency to any other aspect of human life. "The only honest thing to do," says Stanley Fish, who has taken this perspective and would make of it a universal creed of all academics whatsoever, "when someone from the outside asks, 'what use is this venture anyway?' is to answer 'none whatsoever,' if by 'use' is meant (as it always will be) of use to those with no investment in the obsessions internal to the profession."[2] History, on this account, together with the other forms of postmodern academic life, is reduced to the status of a game or of a conversation among members of a private club. How very different in this regard is contemporary history-writing from the various forms of writing—historical, philosophical, and literary—of the Renaissance. As the dedicatory epistles appended to works from that era show, those who then wished to exercise their creativity knew instinctually that they needed a patron, and that the way to gain one was to be useful, either to his vanity, or in some other way to society as a whole or to one of its parts, and to celebrate that usefulness in glowing terms. Galileo, Bach, Velazquez, Racine, Capability Brown, Leibniz, and the list goes on: innovative geniuses all, and all of them highly valued courtiers and public servants. Have the history departments of the twentieth century produced any works comparable to theirs? One

---

2. Stanley Fish, *Save the World on Your Own Time* (New York: Oxford University Press, 2008), 154.

cannot help but wonder whether protestations of autonomy may in fact be a salve for the wounds of neglect.

Historians, even professional ones, have a saving grace, and it is their teaching. By teaching their social role has been most nobly fulfilled in the past—as when the Humanists of the early modern period were the tutors of kings and aristocrats, artists and missionary priests—and still makes noble contributions today. Even when writing for or speaking to a public that is not a school, historians remain teachers, whatever other roles they may also fill. There is never any mistaking the instructive content of the historian's utterance for mere diversion: the formality of calling someone an historian and acknowledging that there is a craft behind his narrative is to raise him above the status of mere storyteller and into that of instructor. Healthy communities make time for their historians to speak, so that they may function as the public voice of the shared memory that binds the community together with its ancestors and offers a patrimony for future generations. And it is always clear that there is too much of the past for all of it to be remembered, too many trivial details best left out of stories and only a small number of essential deeds and characters to be carefully remembered, from which follows the need for the historian's careful exercise of judgment. For a community to tell its story is a mark of its existence; for a community to attend to the office of the historian is a mark of its well-functioning, of its heightened use of reason and its more serious attention to the good. Scientists, artists, and other technical members of a university may find it difficult to teach and much more attractive to inquire, to practice, to make, or to perform, but the historian's inquiries do not open new possibilities for human power over nature, nor do his discourses pack theaters with the satisfied purchasers of high-priced tickets, nor does his practice produce a new generation of captains of industry. The historian, to the contrary, has much in common with the philosopher: he ponders questions, especially old questions, that he thinks retain the power to shape our lives, and he offers the fruit of his contemplation in a mode of moral seriousness. However much he may wish to deny it, his claim to attention comes not from the profitableness of his discoveries, the inventiveness or sheer beauty of his prose, or the novelty of his find-ings, but from the solid weight of his judgment. The historian, at his best, is a model for the virtue of right judgment, and his writing, dis-course, conversation—in a word, his instruction—has as its intrinsic end the diffusion of that intellectual virtue.

To call right judgment an intellectual virtue is to identify it as a firm disposition of the mind, a habit of thinking and of reasoning. In the case of things that are to be done, the ordinary conclusion of a line of reasoning is the decision to act in a certain way and, indeed, the command of that act. Yet a person may reason about the kinds of things that are to be done without commanding the action, and, in this case, the end of the reasoning is simply a judgment. To say that there is a virtue governing judgment is to affirm that it is possible for one person to judge better or worse than another. Prior to the advent of the various characteristically modern forms of sophistry, it was un-derstood that this distinction between the wise and the foolish was real, reliable, and of tremendous social importance. Indeed, the very point of traditional conceptions of education was to form in the young precisely such a habit of right judgment. Montaigne's essay "On the Education of Children" stands as an eloquent witness to that common way of thinking. One may reasonably ask, however, just how such a faculty can be formed by study. Montaigne's answer was characteristi-cally concrete:

> Take Palvel and Pompeo, those excellent dancing-masters when
> I was young: I would like to have seen them teaching us our
> steps just by watching them without budging from our seats,
> like those teachers who seek to give instruction to our under-standing without making it dance—or to have seen others teach
> us how to manage a horse, a pike or a lute, or to sing without
> practice, as these fellows do who want to teach us to judge well
> and to speak well but who never give us exercises in judging or
> speaking.[3]

---

3. "On Educating Children," in Michel de Montaigne, *The Complete Essays*, trans. M. A. Screech (London: Penguin, 2003), 171–72.

Just as a dance instructor insists that his students get off the bench and dance, so also the educator of judgment insists that his students practice their judgment by making judgments, submitting to criticism, reforming, revising, and resubmitting their judgments. As Edward S. Reed aptly declared, refashioning an argument made by Charles Taylor, "One cannot develop and grow through experience into a rich self without embracing viewpoints, defending them against criticisms, and improving or even changing them when necessary."[4]

Further precision on this point of the training of judgment is available in a series of distinctions made by Thomas Aquinas. We are concerned to identify a kind of habitual rectitude in reasoning. With regard to a speculative question—such as, for instance, the question of whether the human soul is by nature incorruptible—rectitude in reasoning will involve a number of habits of mind, including the ability to discriminate among the possible meanings of a term, the knowledge of the canons governing what sort of evidence is rightly taken to be an appropriate starting point for the inquiry, and skill in the use of various sorts of dialectical arguments, including, most especially, the ability to draw out the false or self-contradictory consequences of a rival position. At length, the positive argument for the proposition in question must be put into a valid form, so that it proceeds without false inference from the principles, once those principles have been discovered, defined, and tested against rivals.

Habitual rectitude of reasoning with respect to practical matters is not usually so complex, nor does it so much depend upon training in the art of reasoning. There is, moreover, another principle that is immediately relevant to practical reasoning, which is the disposition of the agent to the good. In a course of practical reasoning—that is, in the making of a decision about something that is to be done or to be avoided—the most relevant principle is the end, that is, the good. Yet a person may be either well or poorly disposed towards the good. The bad man's faulty disposition will warp his judgment; he will liter-

---

4. Edward S. Reed, *The Necessity of Experience* (New Haven, CT: Yale University Press, 1996), 142.

ally see the end askew and make moral pronouncements according to his astigmatic moral vision. The right appetite that comes from moral virtue is, therefore, a necessary precondition for gaining the intellectual virtue of right judgment. Such a moral disposition, however, does not suffice on its own. Practical wisdom, or prudence, is the crown of the moral life, and it is not normally attained by the young. Aquinas indeed acknowledges that good judgment owes something "at its root" to aging, for the experience enjoyed by elders has given them the opportunity to measure their judgments by the actual course of human events rather than by the dreams of their youth. Yet this experience is made fruitful only by the pursuit of virtue, and, to a degree, that pursuit, if well-directed, can take the place of experience. And therefore Aquinas contends that the habit of right judgment can be gained "directly from the part of the cognitive power itself, when it is not imbued with depraved ideas, but with true and right ones."[5] This replacement of erroneous conceptions of the good with true ones is, on the one hand, the work of the speculative part of moral science, that is, the ability to distinguish good action from bad, virtue from vice, and true happiness from false. Yet, it is essential to recall that what is at issue here is the growth of the power of right judgment and not merely the knowledge of ethical doctrine. It is common enough to find men and women of unimpeachable principle, but of hasty, rigid, or otherwise questionable judgment. The task of moral education is not merely to imbue the mind with right doctrine, but also, and crucially, to nourish, to train, and to strengthen the ability rightly to exercise the faculty of judgment itself by the application of ethical principles to particular cases. This forcing of students, or readers, up off the benches and into the dance is the essential task of humanistic education, and when it is done with respect to real examples and not fictional ones, it is the particular labor of the historian.

---

5. *Summa Theologiae*, II–II.51.3.ad1: *directe ex parte ipsius cognoscitivae virtutis, puta quia non est imbuta pravis conceptionibus, sed veris et rectis.* Aquinas also notes the possibility of receiving the virtue as a gift of divine grace.

## Principles of Judgment

When the historian's labor has been specified as the exercise of right judgment upon the data of the past, for the sake of the formation of the virtue of right judgment in his audience, the dependence of the historian's craft upon the science of ethics is clear. The principles of ethical theory—whether philosophical or theological—are the extrinsic principles of the historian's craft. They are as much the starting point of the historian's labor as the principles of medicine are the starting point of the pharmacist's craft. The impetus under which the good historian inquires, considers, speaks, and writes is a concern for the human good. Behind his particular concerns—be they the origins of wars, the course of revolutions, the changing fortunes of a village, a region, a nation, a social class, or a science—lie questions of much broader significance. These questions can be formulated in universal terms: "Is it possible to rule well?" "Are humans better off when they seek equality or excellence?" "What does a single life well-lived look like?" "Is a decent approximation of human happiness a goal that is possible to realize?" "Are human beings made happier by religious faith?" Adequate answers to questions such as these require the data of human experience, the data of history, but they are of necessity framed in non-historical terms, in terms of virtues and vices, conceptions of law, justice, happiness, and community, of eternal punishment and reward, and of man's relationship to God. It *should* be uncontroversial to say that the historical enterprise takes its origin from man's quest for rational fulfillment and that the conclusions—the judgments—expressed by historians about their particular subjects are only as excellent as the ethical principles that frame them are adequate to the task of expressing the truth about human flourishing.

Our interest here, however, is not in the details of ethical judgment—we happily agree with Newman that the Catholic tradition has cast itself into a certain form of thinking on these matters and that the historian chiefly needs to respect that inheritance.[6] Nor does

---

6. John Henry Newman, *Apologia Pro Vita Sua*, ed. Ian Ker (London: Penguin, 1994), 224–25.

our present concern extend to those principles of judgment or canons by reference to which the quality of expositions of any kind are to be discerned: criteria about the use of language, the marshalling of evidence, and the rules of inference that are gained from the arts of grammar, rhetoric, and logic. Rather, in examining the historian's craft, it is our goal to ponder what may be called the intrinsic principles of historical judgment, the principles that relate to the composition, understanding, and evaluation of coherent narratives of past human actions. Those principles we take to be of two kinds: narrative and dramatic.

## The Role of the Master Narrative

All works of history are embedded in some master narrative of human events: either an implicit master narrative or an explicit one, either a true or a false one. Among modern works of Catholic historiography, the most venerable examination of the importance of master narrative is Bossuet's *Discourse on Universal History*.[7] The *Discourse* was the chief part of the historical enterprise that was Bossuet's role as tutor to the Dauphin and is, as Orest Ranum observed, marked by the pedagogical concerns of a "humanist historian" whose "ultimate aim" was to "instruct the reader agreeably."[8] Louis XIV had commanded that his son be formed "for labor and for virtue," so Bossuet attended to those exercises that would make the prince ready to practice "the craft of kingship."[9] Even if history were "useless to other men," he wrote in the opening line of the *Discourse*, it would be necessary for princes. The "prudence that makes them reign well" must be founded upon wide experience, and what better way to gain it than by supplementing their

---

7. An earlier version of the discussion of Bossuet that follows appeared as "'A Study Bearing Fruit Beyond All Price': MacIntyre, Bossuet, and the Historian's Craft," *Fides et Historia* 44 (2012): 15–29.

8. Orest Ranum, "Introduction" to Bossuet's *Discourse on Universal History*, trans. Elborg Foster (Chicago: University of Chicago Press, 1976)," xxiv.

9. Bossuet, *De Institutione Ludovici Delphini* [1679], in *Oeuvres complètes*, ed. Abbé Guillaume (Lyon: Briday, 1879), VII: 379.

personal experiences with "examples from ages past"? Through the study of history, princes can "form their judgment without risking" either their own glory or the well-being of their subjects.[10] Indeed, the importance of history looms large in the plan of studies Bossuet described in his letter to the pope, where, following Cicero, he called it the "teacher of human life" (*humanae vitae magistra*).[11] To train the mind for right judgment requires that judgment itself be practiced, which in turn demands that the appropriate matter for judgment be ready to hand in the form of narrative accounts of human action, such as the classical histories by Thucydides, Polybius, Sallust, and Caesar. Yet these accounts, to be useful, must be true. And to be able to distinguish true historical works from false, there are also principles germane to historical narrative itself. It was Bossuet's concern in the *Discourse on Universal History* to supply just such standards of judgment.

The first of the *Discourse*'s three parts is a narrative of the world from the Creation through the coronation of Charlemagne, which Bossuet entitled *The Epochs, or the Course of Ages*. The function of the epochs is to serve as "resting places" for the mind.[12] The prince, or, indeed, any educated reader, will often be presented with arguments drawing upon past events for their matter. In order to evaluate these arguments, one must be able to situate them within the context of the whole history of the world, so that they "do not become confused in your mind;" that is, one must be able to "avoid anachronisms." The crucial task, as Bossuet repeatedly stressed, is to engrave the "order" of events upon the memory. The epochs assist in this task in the same way that large cities serve as the points from which the map of a whole country becomes intelligible.[13] And, in service of this end, it is crucial that they be few in number; Bossuet employed but a dozen. Those who

---

10. *Discours sur l'histoire universelle*, in *Oeuvres complètes*, VIII:135.

11. For Bossuet's reference to history as *humanae vitae magistra*, see *De Institutione Delphini*, O.C., VII: 350. Compare Cicero, *De Oratore*, II.36a, in *On the Ideal Orator*, trans. James M. May and Jakob Wisse (Oxford: Oxford University Press, 2001), 133.

12, *Discours*, in O.C., VIII:136.

13. *Discours*, in O.C., VIII:135, 172, 136.

have taught introductory courses in Western Civilization can read-ily appreciate his shrewdness. For the teaching of such courses soon shows the instructor that many beginning students have almost no knowledge of history, and that concerted effort is required to build up the solid foundation of a narrative framework against which specific works, figures, and events can be profitably considered. Knowledge of the "course of the ages," once fixed in the mind, serves as a prelimi-nary check on such foibles as sloppy periodization, premature iden-tification of trends, and outright mythmaking. It is this kind of skill in assessing the factual adequacy of appeals to the past or accounts of change over time that gives historians their characteristically critical stance compared to other sorts of humanists.

If the first requirement of an historical narrative is its truthful-ness as a record of the past, the second is that it be set within the context of a true master narrative. The point is the premise on which the *Discourse* as a whole rests. When, in the preface, Bossuet explained that the function of a universal history is to serve as a "general map" within which "particular maps" can be situated and to present "the whole order of the ages" in what amounts to "the blink of an eye," he was building into his account more than mere chronology. For it was the "course . . . of religion and of empires" that he wished to "impress upon" the Dauphin's memory, and that meant, as we might be inclined to say, an intermingling of sacred and profane history. It is in the *Ep-ochs* that this aspect of the work is most clear, for of the dozen resting places for the mind, the two crucial ones are the Creation and the birth of Christ. These two events, especially as they are dwelt upon at length in the *Discourse's* second part, *The Course of Religion*, provide the framework within which Bossuet's historical account unfolds and which the reader is bid to adopt. And although it is the work of the theologian to provide a reasoned account of the significance of these events, the Christian historian must take stock of them in order to exercise right judgment. The historian's choice of beginning and end points of human history as a whole will largely determine, and will certainly reveal, his convictions about the ultimate destiny of human nature and its potentialities for fulfillment. This point is amply borne out, on the one hand by a glance at the secular universal histories of Condorcet, Marx, and Fukuyama, and on the other by Benedict XVI's encyclical letter *Spe Salvi*, which has provided a compelling reflection on the perennial importance of the Creation, the Fall, and the Last Judgment within any Christian approach to human history.

If Bossuet testified to some of the intrinsic principles of the historian's craft, he surely did not testify to all of them, or, at the least, his *Discourse on Universal History* did not seek to provide them. The prominent lessons of the *Discourse* seem to be three: true narratives provided by historians should at least implicitly bear some reference to the beginning and end of the human drama; they should fall into some recognizable relationship to one or more of the turning points in the middle of that drama; they should avoid the more obvious kinds of errors of anachronism. Present in Bossuet's *Discourse* in germ form is also a more substantive point about the importance of narrative: namely, that the search to achieve an adequate master narrative is itself a kind of beginning in the study of history. The point was made particularly well by Hilaire Belloc in a letter to the young Philip Hughes, the future author of a justly celebrated history of *The Reformation in England*. Hughes had written to Belloc, already a widely admired writer, asking him for advice about a course of reading. Belloc in reply insisted that Hughes avoid reading up on the debating points commonly thrown in the face of Catholics—the Crusades, the Inquisition, bad popes, and the like—and instead concentrate on learning the narrative of the transformation of Western Civilization by the Christian faith. "The point is this," he said, "Christendom or Europe was formed and grew up in a particular way. Whether the Catholic Church is true or false has nothing to do with the reality of that formation."[14] Like his contemporary Christopher Dawson, Belloc argued that the proper history of the development of medieval civilization was as much a sociological one as a doctrinal one. In order to understand the creative force of Christianity, he said, Hughes would need to read the primary sources of the Dark Ages, the chronicles of Gregory of Tours, Sulpi-

---

14. Hilaire Belloc, *Letters*, ed. Robert Speaight (London: Hollis and Carter, 1958), 81.

cius Severus, and the like, and read with critical care the prevailing historical narratives that attempted to set the Faith on the margin. The degree to which Hughes internalized Belloc's counsel can be appreciated by the larger divisions of his later work, a three-volume *History of the Church*; his first volume bore the subtitle "The World in Which the Church Was Founded," while the second was called "The Church and the World the Church Created."[15]

To achieve an adequate master-narrative is the crucial beginning, for without having sufficiently reflected upon it, the Catholic historian may unwittingly contribute to some other tradition's master narrative. Yet it should be recalled that the master narrative functions only as a regulative principle or rule in the historian's craft, and certainly not as source of deductive argument or even as its normative expression. Each new generation does not, in fact, require the comprehensive retelling of the story of God's mercy to his people, at least not a retelling that presents itself as new. Every generation has its rhetorical setting; the emphases that sufficed to communicate essential truths at one time may not suffice in another. But it would make a mockery of the historian's craft were every historian expected to produce as his masterpiece a universal history the scope of Bossuet's, or even of Belloc's *History of England* or Hughes's *History of the Church*. Moreover, an undue emphasis upon master-narrative as a principle of the composition of histories risks the loss of a principle of almost equal importance: that the narrative is one of human action and, accordingly, to be adequately presented needs in some way to mirror the dramatic form taken by human actions themselves.

## History as Dramatic Narrative

"What do you read, my Lord?" "Words, words, words."[16] Prince Hamlet's exasperation stemmed from his immersion in deceptive speech,

---

15. See the "Introduction" to the second volume; Philip Hughes, *A History of the Church*, revised edition, vol. II (New York: Sheed and Ward, 1949), v–vii.

16. Shakespeare, *Hamlet*, 2.2.189.

and may succeed in capturing the feeling of the aspiring Catholic historian two or three years into a program of graduate studies. Setting aside the distortion of the past by the unscrupulous, the careless, and the duped, the critical reader is still confronted with the problem of books and articles that seem more fit to clutter the shelves of research libraries than to be read, let alone reread with profit and enjoyment. Any craftsman does well to look at his performance with a full measure of self-criticism, asking why his loaves of bread have not sold like hotcakes, why his chairs sit in the shop floor instead of in a customer's dining room, or why his symphony cannot find conductors wishing to play it. To blame the defects of an undiscerning audience will not always suffice, even to convince ourselves. There are times when the craftsman must be brutally honest: slipshod, uninspired, and unoriginal work has too often left our desk for that "public" we crave when we publish. We should ask why countless monographs from the past half-century find few or no interested readers while the great historians of the past continue to be read, in spite of the fact that their "research" has been surpassed by subsequent scholars? Why does Gibbon still occupy the shelves of bookstores in a Penguin paperback? Why did Paul Claudel—no mean critic—name Bossuet's *History of the Variations of the Protestant Churches* as his choice "if only one book of our literature could survive to bear witness to the world of the French language and spirit"?[17] Why do Belloc's histories, so often hurriedly written and couched in terms so absolute as to embarrass, still find devoted readers? The answer, of course, is that Gibbon, Bossuet, and Belloc all wrote lively, expressive, even graceful prose and, what is more, told compelling stories. Historians owe it to their craft to remind themselves that the material of their craft is words and that their craft itself has something to say about composition and storytelling.

It is to a youthful work of John Henry Newman, *The Church of the Fathers*, that we turn to illustrate the dramatic side of the historian's craft.[18] The work was originally published serially in the 1830s in the

---

17. Claudel, quoted in Gérard Ferreyrolles, et alia, *Bossuet* (Paris: PUPS, 2008), 20.

18. For another, parallel consideration of Newman as an historian, see Christopher

pages of the *British Critic*, and later collated, edited, and to a degree refashioned by Newman after his conversion.[19] The Church Fathers of the fourth century were to Newman models of theological seriousness and of heroic sanctity whose example promised to help the Church of England regain its apostolic character. Yet to propose the example of Greek and Latin priests, monks, and bishops for the emulation of the clergy of the Church of England raised some serious difficulties. Although in Newman's day it had become common to admire the past under the guise of an historical novel, it was one thing to shed a tear for Renzo and Lucia and quite another to take Manzoni's *Betrothed* as a serious blueprint for the renovation of Christian England. And although his was an age characterized by the earnestness of the Evangelical revival, it was also an age in which satire was perhaps just as welcome as forthright preaching. Jane Austen may be taken as characteristic of the type of audience Newman wished to reach: that is, the Austen who once said that "pictures of perfection make me wicked," had mercilessly lampooned Mr. Collins, and had preferred the understated virtues of Mr. Knightley to outward shows of chivalry. Newman warned his reader that the *Church of the Fathers* contained mere "sketches," whose "form and character" he qualified as "polemical." Yet he was just as clearly at pains to avoid offending his reader's sense of how a good story ought to be told as he was eager to put before them such puzzling topics as clerical celibacy and the warfare between the saints and demons. Not only would a careful telling of the story of the saints help to diffuse criticism and to discourage scoffing, it would also make the saints more available as models to imitate. Newman explained that the "frankness" that he would employ in depicting the "lingering imperfections" of the saints would "surely make us love them more, without leading us to reverence them the less, and act as a

---

O. Blum, "The Historian and His Tools in the Workshop of Wisdom," *Logos* 13 (2010): 15–34.

19. For the history of the text, see the Introduction to Newman, *The Church of the Fathers*, with an introduction and notes by Francis McGrath, F.M.S., *The Collected Works of Cardinal John Henry Newman*, Birmingham Oratory Millennium Edition (Notre Dame, IN: University of Notre Dame Press, 2002), xi–lxxix.

relief to the discouragement and despondency which may come over those who, in the midst of much error and sin, are always striving to imitate them."[20] It was in this spirit that he wrote the first four of the ten chapters which eventually made up *The Church of the Fathers*, on Basil of Caesarea and Gregory Nazianzen.

Taken together, these chapters paint a sort of dual portrait of the two friends and saints against the backdrop of what Newman called "a drama in three acts": the Evangelization of the Roman Empire, the rise and growth of the Arian heresy, and the overrunning of the Empire by the barbarians. It was in the second of these three acts that Basil and Gregory played out their roles as "instruments of Providence in repairing and strengthening" the Church. They were builders and rulers, but unlikely ones, because, as Newman explained in one of the work's most enduring passages, they were not indomitable leaders of the stamp of Ambrose or Athanasius, but instead were like "the retired and thoughtful student . . . chastening his soul in secret, raising it to high thought and single-minded purpose, and when at length called into active life, conducting himself with firmness, guilelessness, zeal like a flaming fire, and all the sweetness of purity and integrity."[21] The form that Newman gave to his narrative of the two saints was that of the tragi-comedy, like Corneille's *Cinna*, Shakespeare's *Winter's Tale*, or, perhaps, Austen's *Emma*. The stakes in the drama are high, the possibility of a tragic ending is real, but, at long last, virtue is rewarded, if in a surprising, characteristically Christian way. Basil is the lead character, Gregory his counterpart and indeed foil. The story is one of the tragic parting of friends and the Providential resolution of their difficulties. Basil, his resolve steeled through successive conflicts with the Imperial administration, Arian and Arianizing bishops, and even with his paternal uncle, is shown to have been a man of principle and integrity; his conflict with Gregory—one of his oldest and dearest friends—stemmed from their difference in temperament and, therefore, was to a degree unavoidable. Their story, in other words, had the

---

20. Ibid., ix.
21. Ibid., 29.

makings of a tragedy. With the single-mindedness of a general organizing a campaign, Basil had insisted upon Gregory's appointment
to the episcopacy, but his friend was unsuited to the task and retired
from the fray. Their friendship foundered upon the consequent misunderstanding, and though they did see one another once again before
Basil's death, their joyful camaraderie in the service of the Gospel
had come to an end. Yet after Basil's death, "Basil's spirit, as it were,
came into [Gregory], and within four months of it he had become a
preacher of the Catholic faith in an heretical metropolis, had formed
a congregation, had set apart a place for orthodox worship, and had
been stoned by the populace."[22]

The great advantage that tragic poetry has over historical narrative is in the way individual deeds are portrayed, that is, dramatically: they are enacted. The confrontation of Angelo by Isabella in the
second act of *Measure for Measure*, culminating in her speech against
"man, proud man," does something far better than naming the hero-
ine's courage, it invites us to embody that courage, first in our hearts
by thrilling to the speech as performed, then by speaking it ourselves
(not merely saying the speech, but performing it with proper emphasis and emotion), finally, and crucially, by making it one of the instances in our mind that identifies the mean and the excellence that
is the virtue itself so that it can be accessed as a guide for our own
action. History at its best, however, can accomplish much the same
function as dramatic poetry, and Newman's *Church of the Fathers* does
just that. We pick up the story on the eve of Basil's estrangement from
Gregory, amidst a struggle for control over the Church in Cappadocia
between Basil and another bishop, Anthimus, painted by Newman as
a creature of the Emperor Valens, and a leader of the Arianizing fac-
tion. Anthimus was laboring to undermine Basil's authority within the
Church. "Gregory," Newman related, "at once offered his assistance to
his friend," offering his assistance in the most handsome terms: "'I will
come, if you wish me,' he had said, 'if so be, to advise with you, if the

---

22. Ibid., 76.

sea wants water, or you a counsellor; at all events, to gain benefit, and to act the philosopher, by bearing ill usage in your company.'"

Accordingly, they set out together for a district of Mount Taurus, in the second Cappadocia, where there was an estate or Church dedicated to St. Orestes, the property of the see of Cæsarea. On their return with the produce of the farm, they were encountered by the retainers of Anthimus, who blocked up the pass, and attacked their company. This warfare between Christian bishops was obviously a great scandal in the Church, and Basil adopted a measure which he considered would put an end to it. He increased the number of bishoprics in that district, considering that residents might be able to secure the produce of the estate without disturbance, and moreover to quiet and gain over the minds of those who had encouraged Anthimus in his opposition. Sasima was a village in this neighbourhood, and here he determined to place his friend Gregory, doubtless considering that he could not show him a greater mark of confidence than to commit to him the management of the quarrel, or could confer on him a post, to his own high spirit more desirable, than the place of risk and responsibility.

Gregory had been unwilling even to be made a priest; but he shrank with fear from the office of a bishop. He had upon him that overpowering sense of the awfulness of the ministerial commission which then commonly prevailed in more serious minds. "I feel myself to be unequal to this warfare," he had said on his ordination, "and therefore have hid my face, and slunk away. And I sought to sit down in solitude, being filled with bitterness, and to keep silence from a conviction that the days were evil, since God's beloved have kicked against the truth, and we have become revolting children. And besides this, there is the eternal warfare with one's passions, which my body of humiliation wages with me night and day, part hidden, part open;— and the tossing to and fro and whirling, through the senses and the delights of life; and the deep mire in which I stick fast; and the law of sin warring against the law of the spirit, and striving to efface the royal image in us, and whatever of a divine effluence has been vested in us. Before we have subdued with all our might the principle which drags us down, and have cleansed the mind duly, and have surpassed others much in approach to God, I consider it unsafe either to undertake cure of souls, or mediatorship between God and man, for some such thing is a priest."

With these admirable feelings the weakness of the man mingled itself: at the urgent command of his father he had submitted to be consecrated; but the reluctance which he felt to undertake the office was now transferred to his occupying the see to which he had been appointed. There seems something indeed conceited in my arbitrating between Saints, and deciding how far each was right and wrong. But I do not really mean to do so: I am but reviewing their external conduct in its historical development. With this explanation I say, that an ascetic, like Gregory, ought not to have complained of the country where his see lay, as deficient in beauty and interest, even though he might be allowed to feel the responsibility of a situation which made him a neighbour of Anthimus. Yet such was his infirmity; and he repelled the accusations of his mind against himself, by charging Basil with unkindness in placing him at Sasima. On the other hand, it is possible that Basil, in his eagerness for the settlement of his exarchate, too little consulted the character and taste of Gregory; and, above all, the feelings of duty which bound him to Nazianzus. This is the account which Gregory gives of the matter, in a letter which displays much heat, and even resentment, against Basil: "Give me," he says, "peace and quiet above all things. Why should I be fighting for sucklings and birds, which are not mine, as if in a matter of souls and canons? Well, play the man, be strong, turn everything to your own glory, as rivers suck up the mountain torrent, thinking little of friendship or intimacy, compared with high aims and piety, and disregarding what the world will think of you for all this, being the property of the Spirit alone; while, on my part, so much shall I gain from this your friendship, not to trust in friends, nor to put anything above God."[23]

Thus did Newman through the art of narrative portray the "melancholy crisis of an estrangement" between the two saints. It was a "sorrowful catastrophe" that was resolved only after Basil's death,

---

23. Ibid., 70–72.

when Gregory seemed to receive a portion of Basil's spirit and rededicated himself to episcopal ministry and the defense of the Church.

To those familiar with the subsequent course of the Oxford Movement, and Newman's haunting sermon on "The Parting of Friends," his account of the end of the close friendship between Basil and Gregory may seem oddly prophetic. Newman's collegiate life at Oxford had already included a sufficient number of tensions and struggles to teach him real lessons about the importance of forbearance and to encourage him to seek wisdom and solace in the struggles of the saints of the early Church. The kind of critical engagement with the past motivated by a desire to learn from it that this passage embodies is itself instructive.

The essential facts of the narrative are simple enough: amidst the theological and party struggles of the Arian heresy, Basil and Gregory were divided by a difference of opinion. What Newman has done by the construction of his narrative, however, is to invite his reader to reflect upon the conformity of Christian life to the sufferings of Christ. Our status as finite creatures means that differences in view among humans are inevitable, but when these differences are compounded by conflicts in temperament, the engagement of the emotions, and even lapses in judgment, then the differences may become such as permanently divide those who were earlier the best of friends. Here is historical narrative in which the human drama is at the center.

To say that Newman's treatment of Basil and Gregory is a dramatic narrative is to identify it as a story of virtues and vices, heroes and villains, conflict and resolution, and through it all, of human character revealed by words and deeds. The reconstruction that Newman the historian accomplished with this passage was indeed the reconstruction of the past as it actually happened, because the past, like the present, is at its heart a spiritual drama, in which each and every one of us fights (or fails to fight) to conquer self and to serve the common good. The tools that he used in his sketches of Basil and Gregory were the same tools that he had forged as a student, tutor, and preacher at Oxford. From the close reading and discussion of the plays of Sophocles, Aristotle's *Nicomachean Ethics*, and the Old and New Testaments, Newman had gained a habitual cast of mind in which the human good is both an attractive and a threatened ideal, dynamically sought and imperfectly gained by historical actors and by ourselves. He carried this cast of mind into the writing of history. His *Church of the Fathers*, therefore, is a kind of retort to Aristotle's claim that tragedy is more philosophical than history because it presents the universal aspects of human action shorn of extraneous matter. There is, indeed, nothing to stop the historian from accomplishing the very same end of offering materials for reflection upon the drama that is human life, as Newman does here. And the historian has the considerable advantage of dealing with human actions that have actually been chosen, completed, and subsequently analyzed and discussed. Finally, it is well to notice Newman's care in his own exercise in judgment. Noticing the danger of attempting to adjudicate between two saints, Newman declared that he was merely "reviewing their external conduct," that is, exercising his judgment upon their words and deeds, not those internal dispositions that are the subject of an incomparably higher scrutiny.

## Principles and Practices

We have argued that the historian's craft is most fruitfully understood as the ability to compose historical narratives (and other sorts of works of history, such as speeches, monuments, and reviews) that exhibit the virtue of right judgment by presenting past human actions dramatically and within the context of a true universal history or master narrative. To identify the maintenance of a true master narrative and the dramatic retelling of human actions as the intrinsic principles of the historian's craft, however, is at once to invite the question of whether we are insisting upon the complete redefinition of the historian's practice. Must every outward work of the historian's craft take dramatic form and explicitly contribute to an overall narrative of human affairs from the Creation to the Last Judgment? Surely to give an affirmative answer to this question would be to impose a new and despotic rule upon historians, even those historians happy to understand their work as being in the service of Christ and his Church. It is very far from our intention to attempt to do so. Our task, as we understand it, is to shed light upon principles while leaving the essentially creative task of embodying those principles to others and to subsequent works.

But what do these principles suggest about the practice of the historian's craft? Some sort of initial sketch is certainly in order.

With respect to narrative, what should be borne in mind is the unavoidable role that historical narrative plays in our own moral lives.[24] Our lives are enacted historical dramas, and just as the characters in a tragedy face decisions that are brought upon them by a confluence of circumstances that precede the opening scene, so also are our lives enacted in a given historical setting. Various features of our character, our social roles, and our aspirations are shaped by the setting we have inherited from the past, and our ability to function rationally within that setting can be heightened by attaining a clearer understanding of just what that setting dictates, what sort of choices and creative actions it makes more or less possible or likely. To have a deaf ear to historical setting is much like being a dullard with respect to personal relationships. The person who is ill-attuned to the expectations and characteristic reactions of his family members, friends, colleagues, and fellow citizens will usually act inappropriately. And the person who has not gained a broad and rich sense of human flourishing will act unimaginatively. The same is true, if perhaps less spectacularly, with respect to the knowledge of history. So, for instance, some of the early converts in the Oxford Movement were so enthused about the Catholic history and culture of the Continent that they developed (to some degree willfully) a deaf ear for native English expectations and habits. They may be said to have cultivated a lack of historical awareness, a diminished ability to perceive and to appreciate the inherited culture of their fellow Englishmen. The result was, often enough, gaffes and missteps that led to deep and, in some cases, permanent misunderstandings and arguably slowed the work of evangelization. On the other hand, it was precisely the study of the past ages of the Church and of the Catholic life that existed on the Continent that had

---

24. The discussion that follows is chiefly indebted to MacIntyre's *After Virtue.*

made conversion intellectually possible in the first place, as Newman suggested with the phrase "to be deep in history is to cease to be a Protestant."[25]

Each of us, then, implicitly lives out our own personal chapter of a much broader, even universal narrative. The better we know that master narrative, and the better we understand our place within it, the richer and more finely honed will be our sense of the possibilities that are presented to us for our own choosing. It is the historian's task to help others to understand the place of their lives in the master narrative within which all of us live. He does so, characteristically, both by telling stories and by criticizing stories told by others. There are always many false histories—myths and ideologies of one kind or another—and there are true histories inexpertly told, in which the facts may be adequately presented, but the judgment of those facts is warped or skewed. The historian, then, is a kind of gardener, pulling out the weeds of false myth, pruning the vine of exaggerated judgment, and allowing the flowers and fruit of an adequate narrative self-understanding to flourish.

Although we will subsequently address the question of institutions and practices, at this juncture it should be affirmed that this sort of activity can take as many forms, spoken and written, as it has conventionally done, from book reviews and monographs to popular biographies and textbooks.

A sense of the irreducibly dramatic content of human life, and hence history, similarly leaves the production of the outward works of the historian more or less as we find them. It would be just as absurd to insist that every utterance by an historian look like a Shakespeare play as it would be to claim that a monographic analysis of labor relations in a particular industry, at a particular time and place, could not be deepened or improved by the consideration of the human dramas that were contained within it. There are as many different kinds of valid historical writing as there are authentic human virtues with their at-

25. John Henry Newman, *An Essay on the Development of Christian Doctrine*, 6th edition (London, 1878; reprinted Notre Dame, IN: University of Notre Dame Press, 1989), 8.

tendant practices, institutions, and outward works. To make wooden horse carts was a real excellence, an excellence practiced by and for human communities that sought and embodied common goods. Accordingly, a history of the techniques of the wheelwright can without any doubt testify to human goods and thus encourage and enable their pursuit. Could such a story be told with the same searching regard for the good as Newman's relation of the tragic friendship of Basil and Gregory? Perhaps not with so high a drama: the loss of a friend is, in the last analysis, worse than the loss of a craft technique or guild. Just as *King Lear* and *Phèdre* are tales of kinship and family ties, love and death, and do not turn on the want of a nail, so also the greatest histories have always reposed upon human choice and human character as their principles of judgment and explanation. Yet in *The Wheelwright's Shop*, George Sturt wrote not only an impeccable technical description of a lost trade, but a story of human things, of virtues and vices and of shared joys and sorrows, that amply fulfills the principle that the historian's craft trade in human drama.[26] And what Sturt did for the wheelwright, other historians have done for myriads of subjects.

What we are proposing, then, is a reorientation of the historian's craft rather than an abandonment of its traditional outward works. The services that the historian's craft offers to the communities in which it is practiced are as manifold as differences in genre and audience. It is in the classroom, with the making and evaluating of assignments, the delivering of lectures, and, most importantly the conversation of the historian with his students that the virtue of right judgment—that treasure of the historian's craft—is most directly inculcated. In the many less-obviously pedagogical roles that he undertakes, the historian may simply be manifesting the virtue of right judgment by his argument, or perhaps teaching his audience something about the common good by way of illustration. In any case, his work presents examples of past deeds in a narrative framework for the consideration of his auditors and readers, who stand to gain from

---

26. George Sturt, *The Wheelwright's Shop* (Cambridge: Cambridge University Press, 1923).

that consideration to the extent to which they are seeking in the past the materials for understanding the human good and for enlivening their own quest for that good, either by emulating or by shunning the deeds and characters that the historian has related or by expanding or refining their own sense of the possibilities for creative action that lie before them. When the testimony of generations gone-by serves us by helping to direct us to our final end, it is no pagan fame that the dead have achieved, but the true immortality of the communion of the saints. And by ministering to that spiritual communion, the historian has found the highest possible exercise of his noble craft.

# CHAPTER THREE

# Saints, Sinners, and Scholars

NEWMAN'S ACCOUNT OF THE struggle between Basil and Gregory would not earn him tenure at a major research university. One is much more likely to find his writings assigned in courses on Victorian literature than in history courses on late antiquity or the early Church. Pre-professionalized history writing has largely been consigned to the status of "literature," interesting as a primary document yet unreliable as a guide to the past. Newman's work stands condemned not simply for its partisanship, but also for his focus on persons apart from "broader" issues of social structure and material causation. Is there any common ground between Newman's confessional Christian humanism and the detached empiricism that animates the historical profession today? In this chapter, we will examine the work of Eamon Duffy to argue in the affirmative. A Catholic, Duffy rose to the top of the profession largely through his radical revision of English Reformation history, *The Stripping of the Altars: Traditional Religion in England, 1400–1580* (1992). In subsequent essays and talks addressed to non-academic and, at times, specifically Catholic audiences, Duffy has demonstrated precisely the kind of reflective, philosophical, person-and-community-centered historical thinking that we seek to promote in this book. He has done this, moreover, without sacrificing any of the nuance and empirical precision that stand as the enduring achievement of professional history.[1]

## The Present in the Past

Contra Emerson, all history is not biography. It is, nonetheless, certainly biographical. For Newman as for any modern academic, temperament and life experiences shape the choice of subject matter and style of writing history. For all of its professional trappings, Duffy's *Stripping of the Altars* is also to some degree an extended historical critique of the modern-day stripping that occurred in the name of liturgical innovation in the decades following the Second Vatican Council. This interpretation requires no psychohistory or hermeneutic of suspicion. We have it on Duffy's own testimony. In his essay "Confessions of a Cradle Catholic," Duffy comes clean on the connection between his life and his history writing. He was born in 1947, in Dundalk, a small provincial town on the east coast of Ireland. He describes his childhood as shaped by a Catholic faith almost indistinguishable from Irish nationalism. Though "ardent" as nationalists, his family and neighbors were "observant, but not . . . particularly pious" as Catholics:

> Everyone went to Mass, and my mother and I sometimes attended Rosary, Sermon and Benediction on a weekday evening. Like everyone else, we ate fish on Fridays, we kept the fast days of Lent, we made popular novenas, to Our Lady of Perpetual Succour or St [sic] Gerard Majella at the local Redemptorist church (I was always baffled by the astonishing number of heavily pregnant women in the congregation) and we all had several stabs (in my case uniformly unsuccessful) at keeping the "Nine First Fridays"—Confession and communion on which, nine months in a row, guaranteed a holy death. But there were no col-

---

1.  This and the following chapter were the subject of presentations at the semi-annual conference of The Historical Society, held in Columbia, South Carolina, in May 2012. The authors wish to express their gratitude to Donald Yerxa for his encouragement and support of this endeavor.

lective family prayers in our house. My parents had devotional
books, and owned rosaries, which they used at Mass, but though
I often recited the Rosary and the Litany of Loretto commu-
nally in the evenings, that was at the home of a close friend (son
of the local undertaker) who had a pious mother.[2]

What Duffy's childhood experience of Catholicism lacked in interiority it more than made up for with a robust exterior. The external forms of Catholicism so structured everyday life that even the
impious had no choice but to participate in some manner.

Duffy illustrates the thickly social theology of his childhood
with colorful stories of impious relatives who nonetheless remained
in communion with the Church, both figuratively and sacramentally.
A grandmother whose supposed infirmity kept her from Church (but
not from shopping) would nonetheless receive the Eucharist once a
month from priests eager to spend an afternoon in jovial conversation
with a natural-born storyteller. So too, this old slacker Catholic would
end her evenings at home by praying the Rosary in front of a luminous
statue of Our Lady of Lourdes. Duffy recalls the experience of sleep-
ing beside his grandmother in her big brass bed:

> The sound of the rosary still calls up for me the childhood mem-
> ory of waking to the loud tick of a tin alarm alarm-clock in that
> utterly safe darkness, bathed in the smell of Sloane's Linament,
> and hearing my grandmother's muttered preamble—"This one
> is for Tom, for Henry, for Molly, for Lily"—as she launched on
> yet another decade.[3]

The intermingling of the material and the spiritual in Duffy's
prose reflects a Catholic aesthetic that scholars have identified as the
"sacramental imagination," while the free mixing of the sacred and
the profane in Duffy's childhood suggests the persistence of the late-

---

2. Eamon Duffy, "Confessions of a Cradle Catholic," in *Faith of Our Fathers: Reflections on Catholic Tradition* (London: Continuum, 2004), 11–12.

3. Ibid., 12.

medieval folk religion that Duffy so thoroughly analyzed in *The Stripping of the Altars*.[4]

Duffy's typical, provincial Irish Catholic upbringing has served as the fodder for rebellious Irish writers at least since the days of James Joyce. Still, he writes of it with fond affection. His account of his early education in Catholic schools bears out many a Joycean nightmare—"'God is Love' thumped into you with a stick and a penny catechism"—yet he found in his Catholic education "a world of colour, historical resonance, poetry and intellectual vigour way beyond anything else in [his] provincial Irish upbringing."[5] Duffy moved to England as a teenager, but continued to be educated in Catholic schools, where his teachers exposed him to the most significant of modern secular writers such as Sartre and Camus and introduced him to the modern, historical-critical study of the Bible. Against the grain of his generation, Duffy took exposure to modern thought as an inspiration to explore his Catholic faith more deeply. He attended Cambridge University, where he continued his exploration of theology, philosophy and Church history. Though energized by the play of ideas he experienced in his secular graduate education, he "never encountered anything that seemed half so rich or so satisfying as my inherited Catholicism. . . . Three years of research in church history only confirmed all this."[6]

In the decade or so following the Second Vatican Council, a secular university such as Cambridge may have actually provided a more hospitable environment for nurturing the kind of sympathetic understanding of pre-modern Catholicism found in *The Stripping of the Altars*. Across the western Catholic world, reformers inspired by the so-called "spirit of Vatican II" were quick to jettison much of the de-

---

4. For one representative account of the Catholic sacramental imagination, see Andrew Greeley, *The Catholic Imagination* (Berkeley, CA: University of California Press, 2000). Greeley dedicates the book to the theologian David Tracy, whose concept of the analogical imagination is the foundational theological text for many promoters of the notion of a Catholic imagination. See David Tracy, *The Analogical Imagination: Christian Theology and the Culture of Pluralism* (New York: Crossroad, 1981).

5. Duffy, *Faith of Our Fathers*, 4.

6. Ibid.

votional and liturgical heritage of Tridentine Catholicism in the name of *aggiornamento*. In the world of British Catholicism, what few dissenting voices there were came not from stuffy old priests, but from academic anthropologists such as Mary Douglas, E. E. Evans-Pritchard and Victor Turner, whose study of symbol and ritual among primitive non-Western peoples had only deepened their appreciation for Catholic devotional and liturgical traditions.[7] Though these critics were largely ignored by the Church, their anthropological work had a tremendous influence on a generation of British historians, particularly the neo-Marxists associated with the journal *Past and Present*. These historians turned to anthropology as a key to unlocking the culture of pre-modern Europe.[8] In trying to explain the rise of Western capitalism, many of these historians looked to the organic social and cultural forms of pre-modern Europe as an appealing alternative to the dehumanizing structures of modern industrial society. Scholars who might look down their noses at the Dundalk of Duffy's youth were nonetheless celebrating its historical equivalents in pre-industrial England.

## The Secular Discovery of Tradition

As we have acknowledged the links between Duffy's life and history, it is only fair to take some time to explore how this dynamic played itself out among his secular mentors. By most accounts, E. P. Thompson's *Making of the English Working Class* stands as the greatest single scholarly achievement of postwar British Marxism; by our account, it serves as the most appropriate secular analog to Duffy's *Stripping of the Altars*.[9] As Duffy's work grew out of the crisis in post–Vatican II Catholicism, so Thompson's book and the great social history revolution in scholar-

---

7. See, for example, Douglas's essay on the significance of the Friday meat fast in Mary Douglas, *Natural Symbols: Explorations in Cosmology* (London: Routledge, 1996), especially chapter 1, "The Bog Irish."

8. Keith Thomas, "History and Anthropology," *Past and Present* 24 (April 1963): 3–24.

9. E. P. Thompson, *The Making of the English Working Class* (New York: Vintage Books, 1966).

ship grew out of a crisis in British Marxism: the invasion of Hungary by the Soviet Union in 1956. Up to that point, self-identified Communists in Britain generally affirmed the Soviet Union as representing "real existing socialism." The Soviet invasion shattered any illusions about the nature of the post-Stalinist communism and inspired a fevered search for some authentically socialist alternative to capitalism.

Thompson came to communism through a rather roundabout route. Born to Methodist missionary parents at Oxford in 1924, he joined the Communist Party while studying at Cambridge following a stint in the tank corps during World War II. In 1946, Thompson formed the Communist Party Historians Group along with Christopher Hill, Eric Hobsbawm, Rodney Hilton, Dona Torr, and others. In 1952, this group launched the influential journal *Past and Present*. Even before their political break with the Soviet Union, these scholars had grown dissatisfied with the narrow materialism of the official Marxist view of history. Despite advanced capitalist material development, most of the Western world had not progressed to the next stage of communist revolution. Much like the Italian communist Antonio Gramsci a generation earlier, these historians began to look for the failure of communist revolution in the realm of culture. Superstructure did not simply reflect base. Historical change did not follow from the objective and inevitable development of material forces, but depended upon the guiding, enabling and inhibiting force of culture. This approach existed in an uneasy tension with the official materialism of the Soviet Marxist view of history. Moral outrage at the invasion of Hungary in 1956 led Thompson and others to renounce their Communist Party allegiance, which in turn gave them much more leeway in pursuing their innovative cultural history.[10] *The Making of the English Working Class* is the fruit of that freedom.

Thompson's innovations were two-fold. First, he insisted on re-orienting history away from objective social and economic structures and toward individual and collective human agents acting within

---

10. On British Marxism, see Dennis L. Dworkin, *Cultural Marxism in Postwar Britain: History, the New Left, and the Origins of Cultural Studies* (Durham, NC: Duke University Press, 1997).

history but apart from any preconceived plan such as that handed down by Communist Party orthodoxy. If the Soviet Union was not the natural, inevitable, and desirable culmination of the class struggle, then the historian should not go searching the past for the roots of the Soviet Union. The bracketing of a Soviet teleology opened up to serious scrutiny a much broader range of historical actors and possible alternatives to capitalism. Most significantly, Thompson and his cohort radically reappraised what Marx had dismissed as "the idiocy of rural life," the pre-modern customs and traditions that Marxist orthodoxy had long consigned to the ash heap of history. On this issue, Thompson's treatment of the machine-smashing Luddites in the early industrial era proved to be one of the most influential parts of his book. Against an earlier generation of historians who dismissed them as reactionary enemies of progress, Thompson rehabilitated the reputation of Luddites by understanding their actions as a very reasonable defense of their traditional privileges and independence in the face of growing capitalist technological domination. Pre-modern traditions were thus resources for resistance and occasions for the exercise of human agency against a capitalist vision of historical development.

The sympathetic account of pre-modern traditions in Thompson and other cultural Marxists offered a point of contact between mainstream secular scholarship and Catholicism that Duffy would fully exploit in his *Stripping of the Altars*. This point of contact was, however, far from intended or even apparent to Thompson and his colleagues at *Past and Present*. Anti-Stalinist, the British Marxists retained enough of Marx's secularism to continue to see religion as the opiate of the masses. The pre-modern work traditions that Thompson celebrates appear only tenuously connected to the pre-modern religious culture of England, even when the traditions have names like "St. Monday" (an unofficial day of leisure following a hard-drinking Sunday).[11] Despite or because of his own upbringing, Thompson reserves his most sustained treatment of religion for a scathing indictment of the role

---

11. Thompson, 306.

of Methodism in promoting submission to an oppressive, exploitative industrial work discipline.[12]

Here as in many other respects, Thompson's guide is Max Weber's *Protestant Ethic and the Spirit of Capitalism* much more than any work by Karl Marx.[13] Thompson's revisionist Marxism augmented a more flexible notion of class conflict with a narrative of the rationalization of received traditions and the increasing bureaucratization of traditional social forms. As in Weber, a narrative of pastoral lament for the passing of older ways exists in uneasy tension with a commitment to secular progress. Thompson's perspective is ultimately that of the subject of his first book, William Morris, who sought to combine socialist revolution with romantic aesthetics.[14] Indeed, though historians most often praised Thompson's recovery of forgotten voices of the working class, it is William Blake, not the Luddites or William Cobbett, who for Thompson understood the historical moment of early capitalism most clearly.[15] Rejecting Weber's stoic acceptance of the iron cage of modernity, Thompson nonetheless accepted the material achievements of nineteenth century capitalism as real progress and an essential part of any authentically socialist future.

In his classic essay "Time, Work-Discipline and Industrial Capitalism," Thompson revisited his account of the contrast between pre-modern and industrial regimes of work and leisure with an eye to the development of the Third World. Though he saw in Third World cultures an echo of pre-modern work regimes that allowed more time for leisure, he insisted that the people of Asia, Africa, and Latin America had much to gain from modern Western industrial discipline:

---

12. See in particular ibid., chapter 11, "The Transforming Power of the Cross."

13. For an insightful treatment of how a whole generation of left-leaning intellectuals moved from Marx to Weber in the middle decades of the twentieth century, see Howard Brick, *Daniel Bell and the Decline of Intellectual Radicalism: Social Theory and Political Reconciliation in the 1940s* (Madison, WI: University of Wisconsin Press, 1986).

14. E. P. Thompson, *William Morris: Romantic to Revolutionary* (London: Lawrence and Wishart, 1955).

15. Thompson, *Making*, 832.

"hence would stem a novel dialectic in which some of the old aggressive energies and disciplines migrate to the newly industrializing nations, while the old industrialized nations seek to rediscover modes of experience forgotten before written history begins."[16] Rejecting blueprints and predetermined teleologies, Thompson nonetheless affirms an enduring ideal of social and artistic growth: "there is no such thing as economic growth which is not, at the same time, growth or change of a culture; and the growth of social consciousness, like the growth of a poet's mind, can never, in the last analysis, be planned."[17] Culture has no authoritative claim over us. It is, in the end, merely a resource for the development of creative individuality. For all of its Marxist trappings, Thompson's historical/cultural vision is of a piece with that of an old American Progressive like Charles Beard.

The British historians who wrote for *Past and Present* were no friends of religion. This climate of hostile secularism led one contributor to submit a manuscript charging that the journal had made religion into "a dirty word"; the embarassed editor demanded that he remove the passage.[18] As scholars explored the pre-modern world beyond the work place, it became increasingly difficult to avoid religion; as historians pushed their studies further back into the early modern and medieval periods, religion appeared increasingly difficult to distinguish from what most modern Westerners would call magic. Keith Thomas drew on many of the same anthropological writers as Thompson in producing his magisterial *Religion and the Decline of Magic*.[19] Though exhaustive in its recovery of pre-modern religious practices and popular religious ideas, it shed no tears for the decline of pre-modern culture. Dubbed by one historian "a cultic statement of modernist secularism,"

---

16. E. P. Thompson, "Time, Work-Discipline and Industrial Capitalism," in *Customs in Common: Studies in Traditional Popular Culture* (London: The Merlin Press, 1991), 401.

17. Ibid., 403.

18. Quoted in Michael Bentley, *Modernizing England's Past: English Historiography in the Age of Modernism, 1870–1970* (Cambridge: Cambridge University Press, 2006), 68.

19. Keith Thomas, *Religion and the Decline of Magic* (New York: Charles Scribner's Sons, 1971).

Thomas's book affirms a simplistic Weberian narrative of progress from magical Catholicism to rational Protestantism to secular rationalism.[20] The same material, in the hands of a different master narrative, could produce very different results.

## The Catholic Rediscovery of Tradition

In Duffy's *Stripping of the Altars,* the free mixing of religion and magic, the blurred lines separating the sacred and the profane, become normative, the standard by which to judge the culture of any epoch. Eschewing terms such as "pre-modern" or "popular" religion, Duffy opts for the category of "traditional" religion. For Duffy, traditional religion is not static. Tradition suggests endurance in the sense of an ability to sustain continuity despite change over time. The two-part division of the book—"Part I: The Structures of Traditional Religion" and "Part II: The Stripping of the Altars, 1530–1580"—suggests a division between synchronic culture and diachronic history, yet Duffy's account of traditional structures itself allows for some degree of flux and fluidity. Duffy's argument for the vitality of English Catholicism on the eve of the Reformation stems from his assessment of the success of reform efforts in response to the widespread corruption that had inspired William Langland to write his angry poem *Piers Plowman* in the late fourteenth century. In a time-honored Catholic polemical tradition, Duffy contrasts authentic late-medieval reform with the historical rupture of the Reformation. The first part of the book presents change contained within continuity, while the second half presents change threatening to destroy all continuity.

Still, Duffy's account of authentic Catholic reform is not likely to give much comfort to modern Catholics shaped by the expectations of the Council of Trent and the Second Vatican Council. His first chapter, "Seasons and Signs: The Liturgical Year," begins on a note of discord. After a few opening paragraphs reflecting on the way in which the liturgical calendar structured everyday life in the late

---

20. Bentley, 68.

middle ages, Duffy treats his reader to an almost Chaucerian pan-
orama of the riotous and bawdy activities that accompanied liturgical
celebrations from Corpus Christi processions to Sunday Mass. The
laity made serious devotional decisions through activities that today
would seem little more than carnival games:

> In the parish church at Yaxley there survives a "sexton's wheel,"
> a bizarre roulette-like device with six spokes, each assigned to
> one of the major feasts of the Virgin. Coloured strings were at-
> tached to each spoke and the wheel was spun: the devotee seized
> a string and observed the weekday on which the relevant feast
> fell as a fast in honour of the Virgin through the ensuing year.[21]

This mixing of the sacred and the secular was hardly limited to
the illiterate masses. The Book of Hours reflected a similar "blurring
of the distinction between a ritual and a secular half of the calendar,"
often illuminated with illustrations "for each month not only with
emblems of the principal saints whose feasts occurred then, but with
a picture of the secular activities appropriate to that month—pig-
sticking in December, sitting by the fire in January, and so on."[22] Duffy
acknowledges that some clergy found such mixing of the sacred and
the secular disturbing and even condemned it as superstition. Still,
overall, the Church tolerated the general practices while trying to
contain the worst excesses.

Over the course of nearly four hundred densely printed pages,
Duffy traces this sensibility through the whole range of late-medieval
Catholic culture and finds a remarkable balance and harmony sustaining a multitude of contradictory tendencies within a coherent, organic
whole. By no means a world without conflict, it is nevertheless one in
which existing structures prove more than capable of preserving order in the face of potential chaos. Addressing many topics commonly
associated with Weber's thesis on rationalization, Duffy consistently

---

21. Duffy, *Stripping*, 42.
22. Ibid., 48, 49.

argues against the inexorable triumph of modern rationality over traditional religion. The above example of the Book of Hours, for example, suggests that literacy need not drive a wedge between elite and popular understandings of the faith. In the agricultural setting in which the overwhelming majority of late-medieval English people lived, the literate and illiterate shared enough of a common material life to bridge any gaps created by differences in education. Above all, they shared a common life in the parish, which continued to be the center of social life for rich and poor alike. Duffy acknowledges the increase in private chaplains and private masses among some members of the elite classes, yet insists that the evidence shows that elites continued to direct the vast majority of their patronage toward the parish church.[23] In line with the growth in literacy, reformers of the period encouraged a more interior spirituality among the laity; still, much like the model provided in the great fifteenth-century devotional text *The Imitation of Christ*, this interiority was to reach its fulfillment in the sacramental union with Christ through the Eucharist. The literate and illiterate no doubt experienced the Mass differently, but they shared a common knowledge of a sacred story capable of uniting them across lines of class and education.[24]

Literacy, internalization, individuation—these are all tropes of Weberian modernization. In Duffy's account, however, tradition and modernity appear compatible. Literacy does not spell a retreat from sacramental life. Christianity is an incarnational faith that proclaims the Word made flesh. Literacy simply offers another mode of entering into the mystery of the truth of the Incarnation—though by no means necessarily a privileged mode, since the humblest peasant may possess greater faith than the most learned theologian. In Duffy's account, tradition and modernity fruitfully engage each other largely because tradition sets the boundaries for the modernizing trends present in certain aspects of elite culture. These boundaries were, moreover, as much personal as doctrinal. A sense of rootedness in a parish

---

23. Ibid., 131.
24. Ibid., 118–22.

community, a sense of duty to the ancestors of the past and responsibility for the subordinates of the present—this is the sense of tradition that above everything else kept elites from universalizing the novel, modern aspects of their devotional lives.

The elites who engineered the Reformation in England would abandon this traditional sense of communal responsibility for motives ranging from devotional zeal to a simple lust for wealth and power. In the second part of the book Duffy makes clear that the Reformation in England was at first largely a top-down affair, brutally imposed by elites on an unwilling populace strongly attached to their traditional religious practices. This historical fact established, Duffy provides more than a fair share of blurred battle lines. For all of the ruthlessness of his confiscation of monastic lands and the violence of his repression of those who questioned the legitimacy of the Act of Supremacy, Henry left the devotional and liturgical world of late-medieval English Catholicism fairly well intact. The most destructive stripping occurred during the relatively short reign of Edward VI (1547–53). The even shorter reign of Mary Tudor (1553–18) brought a Catholic restoration of sorts, but certainly no attempt to return to pre-Henrician Catholicism. Partly in response to the Reformation, but partly also in the long standing tradition of clerical suspicion of the "superstitious" aspects of popular devotions, the Council of Trent was in the process of streamlining—if not stripping—Catholicism into a more distinctly modern, rational form. For Duffy, the black legend of "Bloody Mary" has obscured Mary's participation in the Tridentine reforms of the broader Western Church. Though clearly uncomfortable with the fact of Mary's persecution of heretics, his account places her actions in a tradition of repression stretching back to Henry and crossing confessional lines.

Indeed, though *Stripping of the Altars* can be read in one sense as a partisan Catholic history, the overall tone of the book is one of irony rather than indignation. Duffy concedes that by the end of the sixteenth century, the attack on traditional religion had become something of a tradition, and the majority of English people had come to see themselves as Protestants. Still, for all its irony, Duffy's historical argument reinforces the cultural argument that he made in the first half of the book. The English people became Protestant less through a conscious decision on matters of doctrine than through an enduring attachment to their local parish community. At times, community consciousness seems almost like Duffy's substitute for Marxist class consciousness. More than loyalty to Rome, it explains resistance to Henrician and Edwardian reforms; more than attachment to the theological vision of Thomas Cranmer, it explains revulsion at the burnings under Mary. His treatment of the popular response to the Marian persecutions is particularly instructive:

> And however unpopular the burnings were, it would be unwise to assume that all who disapproved of them, or showed sympathy with the victims, were Protestants. Neighbourhood was neighbourhood, however frayed by religious difference and the conflicts of mid-century upheavals. Catholic stomachs too could turn at the smell of scorched flesh, and sympathy for a victim does not necessarily lead one to embrace the doctrine which brought them to the pyre. It is clear that in some communities parochial officials... were at best lukewarm in pursuit of suspect neighbours, but though the archdeacon's men were clearly well aware of this, there is no suggestion that they thought the parish officers themselves were suspect.[25]

Regimes changed, but this sense of community endured. Elizabeth began her reign by reinstating Cranmer's Book of Common Prayer as the foundational liturgical text of a reestablished Church of England. She shrewdly channeled the more extreme elements of Edwardian reform into a tolerance of the Puritan sects, which allowed some aspects of the older traditional religion to survive within the structures of the Book of Common Prayer as it shaped the liturgical life of local parishes.[26]

The victor in Duffy's battle is neither crypto-Catholicism nor crusading Protestantism, but communal inertia:

25. Ibid., 561.
26. Ibid., 589.

> The people of Tudor England were, by and large, no spartans,
> no saints, but by the same token they were no reformers. They
> knew themselves to be mercenary, worldly, weak, and they
> looked to religion, the old or the new, to pardon these vices,
> not to reform them. When the crisis of the Reformation came
> they mostly behaved as mercenary, worldly, and weak men and
> women will, grumbling, obstructing, but in the end taking the
> line of least resistance.[27]

Lest one think Duffy cynical, he goes on to insist that this "conformity was not always ignoble." He concludes by examining the
writings of a local churchman, Christopher Trychay of Exmoor. Living through several regime changes, he "conformed and conformed
again," but "it is hard to see what else such a man in such a time could
have done. For him religion was above all local and particular . . .
his piety centered on this parish, this church, these people." Fear no
doubt played a part in Trychay's submission to the Elizabethan order,
but "for a man like Trychay there was nowhere to be except with the
people he had baptized, shriven, married, and buried for two generations." Duffy's invocation of a passage from Thomas More's *Utopia* ex-
tolling the virtues of such muddling through both dignifies Trychay
by association with the greatest English humanist of his age, yet also
reminds the reader of the nobler standard of martyrdom.[28]

This is all great history, but is it Catholic history? One would not
have to be a believing, practicing Catholic to write a book like *Stripping of the Altars*—but it is surely no coincidence that it is just such a
person who wrote it. At the very least, whatever one wants to call
Duffy's style of history, it is clearly distinct from the type of social and
cultural history spawned by E. P. Thompson. For Thompson, culture
is a resource to be used for whatever purposes historical actors decide
upon in contingent historical circumstances; there are no preconceived limits to decisions and choices, except perhaps the normative
guide of advancing autonomy and control. For Duffy, culture—or the

---

27. Ibid., 591.
28. Ibid., 592.

"structures of traditional religion"—is constitutive, an authoritative guide to action rather than a means to achieve an arbitrarily chosen end. Culture may not be static, but neither is it infinitely malleable. It puts constraints and limits on us that are there to help persons realize their true selves. As a reality principle, a telos of history, the Thompsonian tradition consistently invokes the ideal of the romantic artist; Duffy, by contrast, holds up as a standard the ideal of persons in community, bound together by local attachments in place over time.

Granted, community is to some degree a neutral or at least not uniquely Catholic ideal. Still, pre- and post-Reformation communities are not interchangeable by virtue of some generalized, ahistorical, sociological "we-feeling" that exists apart from any external, transcendent referent. For Duffy, clearly some communities are better than others. Acknowledging the continuity of communal loyalties binding pre- and post-Reformation Englishmen, Duffy nonetheless sees a qualitative decline in the communal sensibility of Englishmen resulting from a decisive break with the past at once social and theological. The Reformation began on the continent with an attack on the principle of indulgences. For all the theological variety among various forms of Protestantism, all Protestants shared a rejection of the Church's teaching on Purgatory. For Duffy, this rejection signaled a shift in historical consciousness: "the Reformation attack on the cult of the dead was more than a polemic against a "false" metaphysical belief: it was an attempt to redefine the boundaries of human community, and, in an act of exorcism, to limit the claims of the past, and the people of the past, on the people of the present."[29]

Written within the conventions of academic history and making no explicitly confessional claims, *The Stripping of the Altars* nonetheless stands as an enactment of the doctrine of the communion of the saints. Though all Nicean Christians can claim assent to this doctrine, the ancillary Catholic teaching on Purgatory and the intercession of the saints gives the doctrine a special prominence within Catholicism, shared by the Eastern churches but lacking in non-Catholic forms of

---

29. Ibid., 8.

Western Christianity. In this way, the Catholic tradition has a special claim on historical thinking among Christian groups. Duffy's career following *The Stripping of the Altars* may be read as an attempt to make good on that claim.


## The Catholic Historian as Public Historian

Published when Duffy was forty-five, *The Stripping of the Altars* was a career-making book that gave him laurels to rest on for the rest of his professional life. A fellow at Magdalene College at Cambridge University, Duffy could have very easily spent the next twenty years directing dissertations that filled in the details of his great work. Instead, he has spent most of the last twenty years trying to translate the argument of *Stripping* into a popular idiom, with best-selling, book-length studies such as *Saints and Sinners: A History of the Popes* (1997); *The Voices of Morebath: Reformation and Rebellion in an English Village* (2001); and *Fires of Faith: Catholic England Under Mary Tudor* (2009). Aside from his efforts to present Catholic history to a non-academic audience, he has published two collections of essays/addresses that show him directly engaging explicitly Catholic and ecumenically religious audiences: *Faith of Our Fathers: Reflections on Catholic Tradition* (2004) and *Walking to Emmaus* (2006).[30] Written with his academic guard down, these shorter works show Duffy at his most confessional, writing as a Catholic trying to find truth in history.

The essays in *Faith of Our Fathers* were originally published in *Priests and People*, a British pastoral journal directed at an audience of lay and clerical ministers. Learned yet accessible, the essays nonetheless strike a tone that might surprise readers of *The Stripping of the Altars*. Duffy appears to have internalized the sensibility of the academic contrarian. In secular academic settings, he is generally sympathetic to traditional Catholicism and critical of modernizing, "progressive" developments; in the Catholic setting of *Priests and People*, he is as likely to offend conservatives as liberals. Many of the essays

---

30. Eamon Duffy, *Walking to Emmaus* (London: Burns and Oates, 2006).

in *Faith of Our Fathers* address topics that have served as flashpoints for the battles between liberal and conservative Catholics since Vatican II. Writing from the perspective of a deep traditionalism, Duffy generally declares a pox on both the houses of conservative and liberal Catholicism. For any reader of *The Stripping of the Altars*, the errors of liberalism are obvious enough; Duffy is at special pains to challenge conservatives to appreciate the novelty of many of the institutional arrangements within the Church that they take to be timeless.

We see this particularly in Duffy's essays on the papacy. He wrote these essays during the reign of a very strong and charismatic pope, John Paul II. With provocative titles such as "Why Do We Need the Pope?," Duffy's essays historicize papal authority and charisma in a way that makes John Paul II seem more of an innovator than a traditionalist. At the most obvious level, Duffy reminds his readers that John Paul's charismatic leadership would have been impossible before the age of mass communication and transportation. Venturing into matters of institutional authority, he informs his readers that the nearly universal papal prerogative to appoint bishops is actually of a fairly recent vintage. In the early centuries of the Church, local councils were far more likely to choose bishops; moreover, through the medieval and early modern periods, popes constantly battled with, and often conceded victories to, nobles, kings and emperors for the right to make episcopal appointments. Throughout these essays, Duffy is very critical of the nineteenth-century ultramontanism of post–Vatican II Catholic conservatives, which with respect to the papacy amounts to support for the papal equivalent of absolute monarchy. He stresses that papal authority was much more limited in earlier times. In "Who Leads the Church?," he stresses that popes were more often followers than leaders of reform movements that began at the local level and received papal approbation only after proving their effectiveness (and, of course, their orthodoxy). In "Rome of the Pilgrims," he deflates the ultramontane cult of Rome by emphasizing that for most of its history, Rome attracted pilgrims by virtue of its shrines to the early Christian martyrs, with the papacy at best a sidelight. Much like in *Stripping*, the common thread of these essays is the primacy of the local Church.

Having offended conservatives by historicizing papal authority, Duffy also challenges liberals who often hold up the local Church as an alternative authority to the papacy. Against the liberals, Duffy insists that the local is not enough. The Church must be unified as the Body of Christ, and, echoing Newman, Duffy insists that this unity cannot be merely "spiritual," but also material, which is to say institutional. The Church without the pope would soon fall into Gnosticism, the ancient heresy that denied the Incarnation and indeed rejected the goodness of the material world. The papacy stands as a check against Gnosticism not because popes have always been wise, holy, men, but simply because they have been men, not disembodied ideas. As Christians have been saved by a person, Jesus Christ, so must they be sustained by a person, even if that person happens to be a sinner. This is for Duffy one of the enduring truths to emerge from the Church's battle with Gnosticism, which was as much about the nature of the Church as the nature of Jesus Christ:

> The Church fought it with ordinariness, making the acid test of Christian belonging not expertise in religious theory or knowledge of secret teaching, but simple sharing in the Church's public worship, obedient attention to her scriptures, and communion with her bishops, the administrators who had emerged as successors to the apostles, handing on their teaching, preaching that old-time religion. The bishops became the public sign that God had tabernacle among real people, that the eternal had entered not into secrecy and the glamour of the arcane, but into the mundane, the public and the ordinary.[31]

Duffy's defense of the papacy challenges both contemporary liberal and conservative alike, but does so from an Incarnational understanding of the Church firmly rooted in a Catholic tradition stretching back two thousand years. His message here has implications for the general practice of history as well. What is the academic history of the past hundred years but a functional Gnosticism, an elite, esoteric

---

31. Duffy, *Faith of Our Fathers*, 62.

discipline accessible only to the chosen few? In the essays of *Faith of Our Fathers*, Duffy breaks out of academic esoterica not simply because of an accessible writing style, but by his placement of himself within a community of shared belief, a community that has authority claims over him regardless of his scholarly expertise. Duffy writes as an insider with a stake in historical issues that are very much alive for his audience, and not simply matters of curiosity or amusement. He does all this, moreover, without sacrificing any of the subtlety, nuance, and sensitivity to historical contingency he developed in his secular professional training.

## Catholic History as the Communion of Saints

The essays in *Faith of Our Fathers* offer one model for a renewed Catholic historiographical practice. Those in *Walking to Emmaus* offer another. In one sense, these are not properly "essays" at all, but rather lay sermons delivered as part of the Sunday Vespers services at the various colleges of Cambridge University. Duffy has much fun at the expense of a practice that has outlived the faith of the vast majority of those who make up the contemporary community of Cambridge. He makes the most of the liturgical setting, however, and manages to transform the genre of Biblical commentary into a reflection on the history of the Church and the nature of our connection to the past.

We see these themes expressed directly in "Let Us Now Praise Famous Men," delivered originally as The Lady Margaret Sermon for the Commemoration of the Benefactors of the University of Cambridge. Much of his sermon is a reflection on the meaning of commemoration. Duffy reminds or informs his congregation that commemoration originally meant praying for the release of souls from Purgatory:

> In fact, that was the main motive for most of the founding benefactions of the University. Certainly it was the one behind the largesse of the Lady Margaret and her chaplain John Fisher, the effective founders of the modern University of Cambridge. The

> Colleges were first and foremost chantries. The return which
> benefactors expected from their largesse was the much needed
> prayers of celibate scholars, many of them engaged in the study
> of theology. Between the poor scholars and the rich givers there
> was reciprocity of need, for the rich had it on the highest author-
> ity that they would enter heaven, if at all, only with extreme
> difficulty, a manoeuvre in fact as unlikely as squeezing a camel
> through a needle's eye. Any help afforded by the prayers of those
> whose studies and mode of life kept them close to heaven was
> gratefully received, and worth paying for.[32]

He wastes no time reminding his congregation that prayers for
the dead ended in the Church of England and its universities during
the reign of Edward VI; he then ponders what possible purpose commemoration has served since that time. The possibilities are not especially noble. With the rejection of prayers for the dead, the reciprocal
relationship between benefactor and beneficiary was lost. Where once
scholars said prayers, they now can only offer praise.

> To whom? Benefactors such as Richard III, Henry VIII and
> George I: Can that be it, then? Does the roll-call of kings and
> queens, dukes and duchesses, lawyers, politicians and million-
> aires ... constitute the meaning of this occasion: a commemora-
> tion of the fact that the University is part of the establishment, a
> canonization of the violent, the powerful and the very, very rich
> who have shared their wealth—in many cases their loot—with
> us and our predecessors? Today is All Saints' Day: are these our
> Saints?[33]

Duffy's question is one that every historian should ponder. Who
exactly are our saints? The modern historical profession has not rejected so much as perverted the idea of the communion of saints, offering both an alternative roll-call and an alternative relation to the
past. The soft populism of so much contemporary social history ap-

---

32. Duffy, *Walking to Emmaus*, 16–17.
33. Ibid., 18.

pears to favor the poor and weak against the rich and powerful, but then re-imagines the poor as those seeking power and control—in effect, struggling to become like the rich. The act of middle class intellectuals celebrating the struggle for autonomy on the part of past historical actors becomes, like the Lady Margaret Sermon, "an exercise in sanctified flattery and self-congratulation, and a devastatingly revealing act of self-definition."[34]

The history of the Lady Margaret Sermon provides Duffy with an occasion for reflection on rival genealogies, rival honor rolls. The endowment for the sermon came as part of the educational reform efforts of John Fisher, "the greatest Cambridge scholar of his times." For Duffy, it is Fisher more than anyone else who "brings together passionate commitment to the University and its institutions, profound scholarship and unchallengeable human integrity. . . . But he is not in our list: instead we commemorate the king who killed him."[35] The same could be said for the historical profession, which continues to privilege, through endless monographs, murderers over martyrs. Henry VIII is a saint in the religion of power, the only authority the modern world accepts.

Duffy clearly delights in exposing the hypocrisy of the occasion, yet this is more than a thinly disguised Catholic polemic. John Fisher may be morally superior to Henry VIII, but he is hardly representative of the Catholics of his day or the Catholics of pre-Reformation England:

> Our medieval forebears were no better than us. They too reverenced success, they too averted their eyes from the vices and motives of the great, they too went fishing for benefactions, and gave thanks when they had netted them. But there was built into the very structure of their commemoration a devastating irony, which undercut and subverted the flattery which they heaped on the great ones of the earth. To pray for the munificent dead was to pay tribute to their success, their wealth, their conspicu-

---

34. Ibid., 19.
35. Ibid., 20.

ous generosity: it was a sanctified form of flattery. But before and beyond all that, it was a declaration that they needed prayer: It insisted that in the one thing necessary, the search for salvation, the moneyed great were not so very successful after all, and the very things that made them great—power, wealth, grandeur— weighed them down and hindered their human completeness. Within their thanksgiving was enshrined an assertion of absolute value, which weighed wealth and power and success against truth and humility and the desire to understand rather than to master the world, and found it wanting.[36]

Praying for the dead is not a substitute for historical scholarship. Still, Duffy here suggests that the humility and sense of personal connection to the past cultivated in this practice are needed for academic history to transcend the worship of technical prowess so prevalent in the modern world outside of academia.

The practice of historical scholarship inevitably bears the stamp of the larger world in which it functions. For all its praise of disciplinary autonomy, the historical profession has long taken its cue from worlds of science, technology, business and politics that have so profoundly shaped the modern West. There is, however, another world outside of academia proper that may serve as a guide to thinking about the past:

At the heart of Christianity and its most fundamental mode of worship lies an act of remembrance, the commemoration of a benefactor. That benefactor is as different as could be from the captains and kings we remember today. In the Christian Eucharist, what is recalled is, precisely, a resounding worldly failure: the gruesome death, outside the city, of a man who ruled no kingdom, made no fortune, won no wars, and who failed to persuade the majority of his contemporaries that he had anything of value to say.

His gift was his own death, a death that did *not* take him to the centre of human achievement. When he came to the courts and councils of kings, it was not as a colleague, or valued servant, heaped with orders and honours, but as a condemned

---

36. Ibid., 21.

criminal. When his message was presented in the Academy, the philosophers and men of letters yawned, and promised that they would hear some more, another day.[37]

As historians seeking to revive a tradition-based historiography in service of the Catholic community, we find ourselves in a similar relation to the Academy. As the early Christians won converts less by argument than by the example of holy lives, so we can only hope to win converts by depicting holiness in ways that are compelling and convincing to a postmodern world all too willing to accept that history is a slaughter bench, a war of all against all in which only the strong survive, until defeated by someone stronger.

Thankfully, there is one historian who is trying to do just this.

---

37. Ibid., 24.

CHAPTER FOUR

# *At the School of the Saints*

OUR SECOND MODEL FOR the renewal of Christian historiography is an unlikely one: a pope. The long pontificate of St. John Paul II accustomed many to the thought that a pope is by nature a teacher and a writer. Yet his teaching came in the form of philosophical and theological reflections and arguments, not historical narratives and interpretations. It is, then, all the more unexpected to be able to look to the Bishop of Rome for an instance of attractive historical writing and speaking. In his addresses at his Wednesday general audiences between 2007 and 2011, Benedict XVI has given a model of the historian's craft that puts the care of a real human community at the center of the historian's efforts, has exemplified the right judgment of the past as the chief virtue of the historian's craft, and has told the stories necessary for the transmission of the virtues that support Christian life. By inviting us to matriculate with him "at the school of the saints," Benedict XVI has made the historian's craft an integral part of his attempt to renew Christian life in our time.[1]

---

1. Benedict XVI, "Saint Thomas Aquinas (3)," June 23, 2010. The pope's addresses are all available from the Vatican website (www.vatican.va) and will be cited below simply by reference to the title of the address, which is usually the name of a saint, and the date of its delivery.

## To Inspire a Love for the Church

Although Benedict XVI's use of his general audiences for the task of speaking about the past is an evident departure from the practice of his illustrious predecessor, it has nevertheless been in fulfillment of John Paul II's own principles and teaching. In a document entitled *Ecclesia in Europa*, a commentary on the synod of European bishops held in Rome in 1999, John Paul II spoke of the Church in Europe as being afflicted by a "dimming of hope," characterized especially by "the loss of Europe's Christian memory and heritage." Pointedly observing that "many Europeans give the impression of living without spiritual roots," as if they were "heirs who have squandered a patrimony entrusted to them by history," he exhorted Europeans to "make a qualitative leap in becoming conscious of [their] spiritual heritage" by "hearing anew the Gospel of Jesus Christ."[2] Since a pope must surely believe that the Gospel is proposed to the world by the Catholic Church, it is, then, understandable that one of Benedict XVI's responses to his predecessor's charge has been a course of historical teaching that has had as its explicit end to invite his auditors and readers to "love the Church."[3]

The central work of Benedict's XVI's historical catechesis has come in the form of addresses at the Wednesday general audiences, which are one of the principal opportunities for pilgrims to Rome to see the pope. During inclement weather, these audiences take place in the Paul VI Hall, which can hold some 6,000 visitors. Otherwise they are in St. Peter's Square, where the assembled numbers can of course be much greater. These audiences unfold according to a highly choreographed pattern, in which pilgrims from the major European linguistic groups are made to feel welcome by the repetition of greetings, prayers, and Scriptural readings in their own languages. After the formal address by the pope, read first in Italian and then in one or more other languages, and the bestowal of his blessing upon the

---

2 . John Paul II, *Ecclesia in Europa* (June 28, 2003), #s 7, 120.

3. "Germanus of Constantinople," April 29, 2009.

pilgrims, there is an opportunity for bishops and other dignitaries in attendance to greet the pope in person.[4]

The catechetical talks that are at the heart of the audiences generally fall between one and two thousand words in length. They are immediately published in each of the major European languages both on the Holy See's website and by its newspaper, *L'Osservatore Romano.* The pope's addresses on the saints have subsequently been republished in book form by Catholic publishers worldwide.[5] These lectures have even given rise to commentaries and study guides offering to make them more accessible to a still-wider audience of readers.[6] On the whole, then, the audiences constitute one of the more notable works of public or popular history of this generation.

Benedict XVI's audiences on the saints have fallen into several different series. Beginning in March 2006, he dedicated thirty-one addresses to the apostles and their collaborators as described in the New Testament. From March 2007 through June 2008, he treated the Fathers of the Church from St. Clement of Rome to Maximus the Confessor in forty-six audiences. Benedict then interrupted his historical series with twenty lectures treating St. Paul during his observance of the Pauline Year, the twelve months from the feast of Saints Peter and Paul in 2008 to the same date in 2009. In February 2009, he resumed his series on the Fathers of the Church, extending it to include a treatment of notable medieval teachers, completing thirty-seven lectures by the end of August 2010. Also during this period he devoted an additional seven audiences to exemplary priests in observance of the Year for Priests. Finally, from September 8, 2010, through April 2011, he brought his reflections on the saints to an end with six-

---

4. Videos of representative audiences can be watched in their entirety on the Vatican website.

5. Publishers of the audiences have included, in the United States, Ignatius Press and Our Sunday Visitor; in France, Bayard, Lethielleux, and L'Echelle de Jacob; and in Germany, Verlag Friedrich Pustet.

6. For instance, Amy Wellborn, *Study Guide for The Fathers* (Huntington, IN: Our Sunday Visitor, 2008), and Mike Aquilina, *Companion Guide to Pope Benedict's The Fathers* (Huntington, IN: Our Sunday Visitor, 2008).

teen conferences on holy women, eight on the modern Doctors of the Church, and a closing retrospective discussion entitled "Holiness." Taken together, Benedict XVI's general audiences on the saints are some twelve dozen in number—not counting the twenty on St. Paul—and in length are on the order of four medium-sized books.

In addition to these catechetical lectures on the saints, Benedict XVI has also written a variety of letters, messages, and addresses that treat historical subjects, usually prompted by an anniversary of some kind or by an apostolic visit to a site in Europe. Noteworthy among these occasional works have been an address at Auschwitz (May 2006), a major discussion of monastic culture at the Collège des Bernadins in Paris (September 2008), two letters on the ninth centenary of the death of St. Anselm (April 2009), several talks during his trip to England for the beatification of John Henry Cardinal Newman (September 2010), and his message to the President of Italy for the sesquicentennial celebration of the unification of Italy (March 2011). Against the background of his major addresses at Regensburg and Berlin and his three encyclicals, these historical reflections show the pope to be actively engaging the crisis of European identity identified by John Paul II.

## Reclaiming a Patrimony

In the 2006 volume *Without Roots*, co-written with Italian senator Marcello Pera, Benedict XVI declared that at "the hour of its greatest success, Europe seems hollow, as if it were internally paralyzed by a failure of its circulatory system that is endangering its life, subjecting it to transplants that erase its identity."[7] At stake in this crisis of identity is both a loss of vitality, as manifested in Europe's low birthrate, and the tendency of immigrants to Europe to belong to one or another non-Christian religion, especially Islam. In the face of the changing religious complexion of European society, to propose that Europe regain

---

7. Joseph Ratzinger and Marcello Pera, *Without Roots: The West, Relativism, Christianity, Islam* (New York: Basic Books, 2006), 66.

her Christian roots is not at all a "nostalgic battle in the 'rearguard' of history," but instead an effort to take "seriously our tremendous responsibility for humanity today."[8] The pope's conviction is that without its Christian identity, not only will Europe as we know it cease to exist, but more importantly, the conscience of the whole world will be darkened to the degree that Europe fails in its mission to testify to the most important truths about God and man.

In response to this crisis, Benedict XVI has dedicated much effort to the challenge of re-evangelization, and especially that of Europe.[9] In doing so, he has been careful to make the distinctions that are necessary for rightly understanding this aim. On the one hand, there can be no easy identification of Christianity with Europe, because "Christianity did not begin in Europe" and so "cannot be classified as a European religion."[10] Benedict XVI is, to be sure, keenly aware of the fact that the Catholic Church is growing in Africa and the East while it is shrinking in Europe and the West. But on the other hand, the Church cannot abandon Europe entirely, because Europe itself "is not a continent that can be defined solely in geographic terms but is rather a cultural and historical concept."[11] Not only is this conceptual or cultural Europe increasingly the form taken by the modern world around the globe, it is also irreducibly linked to Christianity: "It was precisely in Europe that Christianity took on its most efficacious cultural and intellectual form," producing, among other monuments, the great medieval cathedrals, acknowledged by tourists from around the world as "one of the loftiest expressions of universal civilization."[12] From the Christian perspective, Europe's role in human history is irreducibly

---

8. Joseph Ratzinger, *Christianity and the Crisis of Cultures*, trans. Brian McNeil (San Francisco: Ignatius Press, 2005), 31–32.

9. See, for instance, the discussion in Benedict XVI's apostolic letter *Ubicumque et Semper* establishing the Pontifical Council for Promoting the New Evangelization (September 21, 2010).

10. Ratzinger, *Christianity and the Crisis of Cultures*, 29.

11. Ratzinger and Pera, *Without Roots*, 52.

12. Ratzinger, *Christianity and the Crisis of Cultures*, 29, and Benedict XVI, "The Cathedral from the Romanesque to the Gothic Architecture: The Theological Background," November 18, 2009.

providential. At Regensburg, Benedict XVI quoted the prologue of St. John's Gospel, "In the beginning was the *logos*, and the *logos* is God," adding the commentary: "the encounter between the Biblical message and Greek thought did not happen by chance;" during his visit to Paris, he underscored this point by writing the same words of St. John in the ceremonial guest book of the Institut de France.[13]

While his conception of Europe and of its perennial importance to the modern world is firmly grounded in his Christian faith, Benedict XVI has also employed the language of contemporary politics in explaining the same point. Thus he has affirmed the "values of human dignity, freedom, equality, and solidarity" and the "fundamental principles of democracy and law" both as values that Christians can share and as "crucial to European identity." And, somewhat more controversially today, he has warned that in the impending loss of traditional marriage within European society "we are facing a dissolution of the image of humankind bearing consequences that can only be extremely grave."[14] In the face of widespread acceptance of the practices his predecessor called the Culture of Death, Benedict XVI's constant plea has been for secular society to listen again to the great "cultural heritage" of Europe, the "three-way encounter" between Jerusalem, Athens, and Rome that "shaped the inner identity of Europe."[15] As part of that plea, the pope has argued trenchantly from common experience and premises that natural reason can accept. Yet his office is not to be a public philosopher, and so his fundamental contribution to the crisis of European identity has been to preach anew the Gospel of Jesus Christ.

Once again following the example of his predecessor, Benedict XVI has given his office a markedly apostolic character, using it to re-introduce the world to Christ. But whereas John Paul II began his pontificate with an encyclical on the person of Christ himself—

---

13. Benedict XVI, "Faith, Reason, and the University: Memories and Reflections," address at the University of Regensburg, September 12, 2006.

14. Ratzinger and Pera, *Without Roots*, 76–77.

15. Benedict XVI, "The Listening Heart: Reflections on the Foundations of Law," address before the German Bundestag in Berlin, September 22, 2011.

*Redemptor Hominis*—and preferred to approach the tasks of teaching and preaching through general considerations on such topics as the Eucharist, the Rosary, the significance of Sunday, and a variety of topics in moral theology, Benedict XVI has shown a marked predilection for the telling of stories, and especially for reflecting upon the lives of saints. Why? Because, as he explained, Christ is encountered in his Church: "We cannot have Jesus without the reality he created and in which he communicates himself. Between the Son of God-made-flesh and his Church there is a profound, unbreakable, and mysterious continuity by which Christ is present today in his people."[16] To enunciate this principle, however, is immediately to invite a practical objection based upon the widespread unpopularity of the Church in the developed West. If Jesus can only be encountered in the Church, then the obstacles that stand in the way of people loving the Church must be contended with. It is precisely because of the barriers of ignorance, prejudice, and fear and, tragically, some grave barriers of personal injury standing between many modern people and the Roman Catholic Church that Benedict seems to have chosen to reintroduce people to the Church by inviting them to become acquainted with the saints. "The Church lives in people, and those who want to know the Church better, to understand her mystery, must consider the people who have seen and lived her message, her mystery. In the Wednesday Catechesis I have therefore been speaking for some time of people from whom we can learn what the Church is."[17]

## A Papal Proposal for a Renewed Hagiography

To the professional historian, the saints can be a stumbling block. During their own lives, saints are often public commodities, crucial to the integrity of the communities in which they live and indispensable to the lives of those they touch. Not only are memories of them after their death likely enough to be rose-colored, but even the way

---

16. "Christ and the Church," March 15, 2006.
17. "Ambrose Autpert," April 22, 2009.

in which others speak about them during their lives may be extraordinarily deferential. How is the historian able to gain any confidence that he has attained the personality of the saint, and especially of a saint from an era for which documentation is scant? Then there are the more-or-less evident hazards that stand in the way of satisfactory presentation: legends, miracles, deeds of extraordinary virtue, and speech characterized by a directness about spiritual things that most of us would not dare to employ in our ordinary lives. The saints are an imposing lot. It is hardly surprising that most historians—even Catholic historians—find it easier to pass them by.[18]

Benedict XVI's general audiences, therefore, may be seen as a kind of proposal to historians, a sort of leading-by-the-hand to a more courageous embrace of one of the more difficult tasks of their craft. The shape that his proposal takes is a surprising one. The pope is neither triumphalistic, pugilistic, grandiloquent, or prematurely synthetic, but instead patient, concrete, and pedagogically astute. The reader of his general audiences will find few miracle stories, but many invitations to deeper prayer; few narratives of heretics confuted, rebellious kings subdued, or pagan temples cleansed, but many references to charitable work with the poor; few references to ecstatic visions and spiritual gifts, but many instances of the labor of reason and the discipline of the will in the attempt to discern the mind of God. His summary point about Gregory of Nyssa may be taken to exemplify his general practice: the "most important lesson" for us to learn from Gregory is that "total human fulfillment consists in holiness, in a life lived in the encounter with God, which thus becomes luminous also to others."[19] The saints, in other words, enable us to see Christ because they show us the beauty of a life transformed by grace.

What might be called the Augustinian humanism of the pope's hagiography is a direct response to the need to "show a Christian

---

18. There are notable exceptions. See, for instance, Robert L. Wilken, "The Lives of the Saints and the Pursuit of Virtue," in *Remembering the Christian Past* (Grand Rapids, MI: Eerdmans, 1995), 121–44, as well as Wilken's *Spirit of Early Christian Thought: Seeking the Face of God* (New Haven, CT: Yale University Press, 2003).

19. "Saint Gregory of Nyssa (I)," August 29, 2007.

model of life that offers a livable alternative to the increasingly vacuous entertainments of leisure-time society."[20] Across the audiences as a whole, three characteristics of this "Christian model of life" are particularly striking: its clarity of mind, its healthfulness of personality, and its generosity toward others.

Truth is the good of the mind, and the saints show us the pursuit of truth at its keenest. From Justin Martyr, who demonstrates the "ancient Church's forceful option for philosophy, for reason, rather than for the religion of the pagans," to St. Pius X, who founded the Pontifical Biblical Institute for the sake of "fostering a scientific examination of Revelation consonant with the Tradition of the Church," Benedict XVI's saints tell the story of the Christian quest for knowledge and wisdom.[21] In the early centuries of the Church, that quest was deeply indebted to Greek philosophy. The Greek Fathers, such as Clement of Alexandria, are models for those who are inspired to follow John Paul II's call "to recover and express to the full the metaphysical dimension of the faith."[22] The Fathers' medieval heirs, such as Albert the Great and Aquinas, show us that there is no need to fear conflicts between science and religion and therefore encourage us to embrace the task of reasoning to the full. Aquinas, in particular, offers us "a broad and confident concept of human reason" bolstered by a faith that "protects reason from any temptation to distrust its own abilities, stimulates it to be open to ever broader horizons, [and] keeps alive in it the search for foundations."[23] He is, therefore, an example of the engagement with the "whole breadth of reason" that Benedict XVI called for in his Regensburg Address, and the very antithesis to the closed-in secularism that the pope likened to a "concrete bunker with no windows" in his remarks at the Bundestag during his return to Germany several

---

20. Ratzinger and Pera, *Without Roots*, 125.
21. "Saint Justin, Philosopher and Martyr," March 22, 2007, and "Saint Pius X," August 18, 2010.
22. "Clement of Alexandria," April 18, 2007, quoted John Paul II, *Fides et Ratio*, #105.
23. "Saint Thomas Aquinas (II)," June 16, 2010. See also "Saint Albert the Great," March 24, 2010.

years later.[24] Modern secularism, on Benedict XVI's account, is setting itself up to replay the fall of antique paganism before the hardy search for truth of the early Christians, a defeat that was "inevitable" because "it was a logical consequent" of paganism's "detachment of religion ... from the truth of being."[25] Christians can work to secure the defeat of secularism by following the saints' example of the glad and courageous search for truth.

It is not only excellence of mind that the saints display for us, however, but also excellence of will, by showing us healthy, successful, and happy lives. In this connection, one of the more striking passages in his general audiences is the discussion of St. Joseph Cafasso, a priest who lived a hidden life as a spiritual director and administrator in nineteenth-century Turin. He is best known for having been the mentor of St. John Bosco, the indefatigable apostle to Italian orphans and wayward youth and founder of the Salesian order. Bosco was one of dozens of men guided to a deeper understanding of priestly life by Don Cafasso, who taught moral theology and served as a spiritual director at the "Convitto Ecclesiastico," a kind of training academy for priests in Turin. Bosco testified that Don Cafasso's teaching was characterized by "calmness, wisdom, and prudence." He enjoyed the peace of soul that comes from "profound and prolonged prayer," and, as Benedict XVI explained, his very presence "did good" because "it reassured, it moved hearts hardened by the events of life and above all it enlightened and jolted indifferent consciences." Particularly striking is the pope's account of how Don Cafasso's own self-mastery was the foundation of his generosity and effectiveness as a teacher and mentor:

> In all the fundamental decisions of his life St. John Bosco had St. Joseph Cafasso to advise him, but in a very specific way: Cafasso never sought to form Don Bosco as a disciple "in his own image and likeness," and Don Bosco did not copy Cafasso; he imitated Cafasso's human and priestly virtues ... but according to his

---

24. "The Listening Heart," September 22, 2011.
25. "Saint Justin, Philosopher and Martyr," March 21, 2007.

> own personal disposition and his own specific vocation; a sign
> of the wisdom of the spiritual teacher and of the intelligence
> of the disciple: the former did not impose himself on the latter
> but respected his personality and helped him to interpret God's
> will for him.[26]

Those of us who are teachers can appreciate the wisdom of Benedict's commentary; surely the sternest test of the teacher—and of the parent—is the very one that Don Cafasso passed with flying colors. The vignette is impressive as a concrete example that penetrates to the heart of what it means to be a psychologically healthy human being: to be free to serve the authentic good of others. And as a representative choice of Benedict XVI's hagiography, it discloses the criteria of judgment that he employed as an historian.

Finally, the saints show us that the ardent search for God does not separate Christians from their fellow men, but instead impels them to concrete charitable works. This point was a central one in Benedict XVI's pontificate; it is stressed in two of his encyclicals, *Deus Caritas Est* (2006) and *Caritas in Veritate* (2009). In the audiences, he tended to emphasize the way in which charitable work compliments or fulfills the search for God of scholars, teachers, and contemplative religious. Thus he praised St. Augustine for having laid aside his manuscript on the Trinity in order to write more broadly accessible works, noted that Pope Leo the Great was "devoted to the service of truth in charity . . . as both theologian and pastor," and pondered the "lesson" taught by St. Isidore of Seville's successful "synthesis of a life that seeks contemplation of God, dialogue with God in prayer and in the reading of Sacred Scripture, as well as action in the service of the human community and of our neighbor."[27] The point surely resonates with the pope's own experience as a churchman. When discussing St. Augustine, whom he called "a figure to whom I feel closely linked because of the role he has had in my life as a theologian, priest, and

---

26. "Saint Joseph Cafasso," June 30, 2010.

27. "Saint Augustine of Hippo (4)," February 20, 2008; "Saint Leo the Great," March 5, 2008; "Saint Isidore of Seville," June 18, 2008.

Pastor," he emphasized the importance of Augustine's realization that "only by living for others, and not simply for his private contemplation, could he really live with Christ and for Christ."[28] Yet the pope not only discussed the importance of the contemplative and the intellectual being called forth from solitude and repose—as he did also in the cases of Cassiodorus, Peter Damian, and St. Catherine of Bologna—but also he repeatedly stressed the synthesis of spirituality and outward works in saints who were essentially dedicated to the active life. St. Basil and St. Elizabeth of Hungary, for instance, lived exemplary Christian lives in leadership positions, the one as bishop, the other as queen. And during his observance of the Year for Priests, Benedict XVI celebrated Saints Leonard Murialdo and Joseph Cottolengo, noting that these two noteworthy laborers in charitable works had "carried out their ministry with the total gift of their lives to the poorest, the neediest, and the lowliest, always finding the deep roots, the inexhaustible source for their action in their relationship with God."[29]

## Seeking God with the Cappadocian Fathers

The artfulness of Pope Benedict's historiography can be appreciated by comparing his six essays on the Cappadocian Fathers—Saints Basil, Gregory of Nazianzen, and Gregory of Nyssa—with Newman's chapters on them in *The Church of the Fathers*. Both writers are engaged in a work of conscious retrieval; both look to the Fathers of the fourth century because, as Benedict XVI puts it, they are "full of ideas for reflection and teachings that are also relevant for us today."[30] Both writers, moreover, are especially keen to bring the reader into the hidden recesses of the souls of these deep and thoughtful men.

Their chosen means to accomplish their similar ends, however, are very different. For Newman, the age of the Fathers was—like every age of human history—one of "conflict, and of vicissitude amid

---

28. "Saint Augustine of Hippo (5)," February 27, 2008.
29. "Saint Leonard Murialdo and Saint Joseph Cottolengo," April 28, 2010.
30. "Saint Basil (2)," August 1, 2007.

the conflict."[31] As we have noted, he wanted to attract his readers to the saints by showing them engulfed in the drama of life and working out their salvation in fear and trembling. He would rather depict actions than describe characters, and so preferred to "sketch the history" of Basil and Gregory's friendship rather than analyze it.[32] His essays, accordingly, transmit an ambiance rather than argue for a point or lay out a doctrine.

Hemmed in by the brevity of the general audience address as a genre, Benedict XVI took a different tack. Each of his six lectures leaves the reader with a single point upon which to reflect, a point illustrated sometimes by vignettes from the lives of the saints, but usually by quotations from their works. The three men emerge as certain types: Basil of the administrator and leader, Gregory Nazianzen of the poet and orator, Gregory of Nyssa of the speculative thinker. For each of the three figures, Benedict gave one reflection upon his life followed by a second devoted to his works. Together, the six addresses form a certain whole—as the pope himself noted—and present a composite picture of Christian excellence.

In the case of St. Basil, the pope emphasized the clarity of his mind and rectitude of his will. Praising the great bishop for "the holiness of his life, the excellence of his teaching, and the harmonious synthesis of his speculative and practical gifts," Benedict stresses his "wise balance" and the right ordering of his endeavors, the order of the great commandment to love God and neighbor. This was a man who "spent himself without reserve" and was marked by a generosity toward his flock.[33] The overall lesson to be learned from him is the universal one that "life is a stewardship of the goods received from God."[34]

Whereas Basil, the founder of hospitals and dogged opponent of heresy, represents the nobility of the active life when rightly ordered to the love of God, the two Gregories show us the perfection of the

---

31. Newman, *Church of the Fathers*, Birmingham Oratory Millennium Edition (Notre Dame, IN: University of Notre Dame Press, 2002), 1.

32. Ibid., 51.

33. "Saint Basil (1)," July 4, 2007.

34. "Saint Basil (2)," August 1, 2007.

interior life. In Nazianzen, we meet a poet with a "refined and sensitive soul," a man of "profound interiority" to whom nothing seemed greater than "to lead a life that transcends the visible."[35] In Gregory of Nyssa there is a similar thirst for God, but perhaps expressed less affectively and more in terms of the search for truth: "the supreme goal to which all his work as a theologian was directed," says Benedict, was "not to engage his life in vain things but to find the light that would enable him to discern what is truly worthwhile."[36] Yet these are emphases, not differences; for both men, the encounter with God in prayer was both the heart of their existence and their chief witness to us today. Nazianzen's understanding of the end of the intellectual life was abundantly clear: "It was precisely our mind and our reason that needed and needs the relationship, the encounter with God in Christ."[37] And, by the same token, Gregory of Nyssa plainly held the primacy of charity: the soul's good, he said, "is not a question of knowing something about God but of having God within."[38]

Benedict XVI's six lectures on the Cappadocian Fathers conform to the type of his general audiences on the saints. They are essentially invitations to study and, indeed, to live in communion with the saints. It is perhaps not inappropriate to suggest that the addresses display a certain classicism, both because they are rhetorically reserved and because in them the pope seems particularly to have striven for clarity of expression. By customarily restricting his audience addresses to a single point, he has made it easier for his readers to take with them a thought with which to prompt further reflection. In this way, he has given us an example of the historian's craft put in the service of his community, the community of the Catholic Church.

---

35. "Saint Gregory Nazianzen (1)," August 8, 2007.

36. "Saint Gregory of Nyssa (1)," August 29, 2007.

37. "Saint Gregory Nazianzen (2)," August 22, 2007.

38. "Saint Gregory of Nyssa (2)," September 5, 2007.

## To Tell the Story of the Church

In addition to offering a model for a renewed hagiography, Benedict XVI's general audiences on the saints, when taken together as a whole, are a powerful retelling of the Church's own story. As such, they are an encouragement for Christian historians—and, of course, especially Catholic historians—to reclaim the story of Christian civilization as essentially a comic, that is, a happy one. The central theme of the pope's overall narrative is that shared Christian life—Christian culture—was built by the prayer and works of mercy of the saints and their collaborators. At the center of his story is St. Benedict himself. Reminding his audience that St. Benedict is "the patron of my pontificate," the pope declared: "the Saint's work and particularly his Rule were to prove heralds of an authentic spiritual leaven which . . . changed the face of Europe following the fall of the political unity created by the Roman Empire, inspiring a new spiritual and cultural unity, that of the Christian faith shared by the peoples of the Continent. This is how the reality we call "Europe" came into being."[39]

Running as a thread through the audiences are the lives of monks and nuns. There are the monks and nuns one would expect to see, such as Jerome, Benedict, Bede, Bernard, and Gertrude the Great. Yet also present in Benedict XVI's narrative are many other monks and nuns who are less well-known: Ambrose Autpert, Rabanus Maurus, Richard and Hugh of St. Victor, Rupert of Deutz, and the German Benedictine Matilda of Hackeborn. From what he called the "life-giving humus" of "prayer and contemplation," these monks and nuns were able to found and perpetuate not only monastic communities, but also workshops, schools, hospitals, and all the other complex human realities that accompanied the rise of civilization in the early medieval period.[40] Some of the central figures in this story are St. Columban, an Irish monk whose "sense of Europe's cultural unity" led him to extraordinary missionary work on the Continent, St. Boniface,

---

39. "Saint Benedict of Norcia," April 9, 2008. See also his first general audience, of April 27, 2005, in which he reflects upon his choice of the papal name Benedict.
40. "Saint Matilda of Hackeborn," September 29, 2010.

an Englishman who planted the "Christian roots of Europe" by uniting Germany to the West, and the holy French abbots of the Order of Cluny, who bequeathed a "rich cultural and religious heritage" to Europe.[41]

These monks did not, however, set out to build a civilization. Rather, as the pope stressed in his substantial meditation on monasticism delivered at the Collège des Bernadins in Paris, they set out first to "seek God," the God who has spoken through his Son, and within the context of that search and by an "inner necessity," they built a "culture of the Word" of enduring strength and beauty.[42] His implicit master-narrative of the rise of European civilization is a story that puts friendship with Christ—lived and expressed through prayer and liturgy—at the center.

This master-narrative of Christian civilization is, it seems, Pope Benedict's greatest challenge to the Christian historian. It is worth pondering that in many of his addresses on the Doctors of the Church, Benedict chose to underscore the vital necessity for theologians that they first love the Word of God and then listen to it attentively and with humility.[43] Moreover, both in his audiences and in numerous statements to Catholic educators, he has stressed the importance of what he has called "intellectual charity," perhaps best illustrated by this statement about St. John Chrysostom: "Intimacy with the Word of God, cultivated in his years at the hermitage, had developed in him an irresistible urge to preach the Gospel, to give others what he himself had received in his years of meditation."[44] Or, again, by way of contrast, his choice of praise for St. Gregory of Nyssa is revealing: "he developed theology's fundamental directions, not for an academic theology closed in on itself, but in order to offer catechists a reference system to keep before them in their instructions, almost as a frame-

---

41. "Saint Columban," "Saint Boniface," "The Order of Cluny,"

42. Benedict XVI, "Address" at the Meeting with Representatives from the World of Culture, Collège des Bernadins, Paris, September 12, 2008.

43. See, for instance, "Origen of Alexandria: The Thought," May 2, 2007, and "Saint Gregory the Great (2)," June 4, 2008.

44. "Saint John Chrysostom (I)," September 19, 2007.

work for a pedagogical interpretation of the faith."[45] When, therefore, he noted that to the Church historian Eusebius, "historical analysis is never an end in itself," the implication is sufficiently plain: historians, like theologians, are asked to remember that intellectual charity requires that "timidity in the face of the category of the good" be thrown off and replaced by a determination "to lead [others] to truth" as "an act of love."[46] In concrete terms, that means using the historian's craft to invite people to love the Church so that they will be able to find and draw closer to Christ.

## A Reflection

It is well known that a prolonged series of general audiences early in the pontificate of John Paul II has inspired a tremendous interest in what is now commonly referred to as the theology of the body. The voices are neither few nor insignificant who see in this theological emphasis great promise for the New Evangelization that the popes have called for. Might Benedict XVI's general audiences on the saints lead to a similar creative burst of Catholic historiography? There are some notable obstacles standing in the way of such a result, and not only from the complexion of the historical profession itself. The addresses themselves are by their nature episodic. Unlike John Paul II's addresses, they have a chronological rather than a conceptual ordering. And while certain themes are manifestly central to Benedict XVI's talks on the saints, the master-narrative that undergirds it does remain largely implicit, or, at the very least, only emerges with clarity when the addresses are read sequentially and in concert with some of his other writings. Finally, there is the problem of genre. As occasional works, the addresses fail to have the impact that is enjoyed by a papal encyclical, nor do they bear significant weight as expressions of the

---

45. "Saint Gregory of Nyssa (I)," August 29, 2007.

46. "Eusebius of Caesarea," June 13, 2007; Address at the Meeting with Catholic Educators at the Catholic University of America, April 17, 2008. See also Benedict XVI's homily at his Celebration of First Vespers with the University Students of Rome, at the Vatican, December 17, 2009.

teaching authority of the Church. As a result, they risk being ignored by the Catholic world.

In light of these challenges, it seems all the more clear that it is wise to take Benedict XVI's general audience addresses on the saints less as a finished work of history and more as an historiographic challenge to Catholic historians. It is for them to find new and effective ways to embody the pope's insights and teachings and to make them available to other audiences.

CONCLUSION

# In The Workshop of the Past

IN OUR REFLECTION UPON how Catholic historians might renew their craft, we have consistently stressed what we take to be the essential or intrinsic qualities of the craft rather than its output or characteristic works, and with good reason. If, as we contend, the products of the historian's craft are works that seek to help particular communities in their common pursuit of the good life, then the historian's work necessarily unfolds within a particular context and will necessarily be most useful within context. But as contexts vary enormously, so then will the historian's outward works be many and different. In this regard, the historian's work has something in common with the poet's: just as the poet's task may be said to be that of tuning the ears of his contemporaries so that they might more readily attend to the nuances of language, so also the historian calls upon his audience to bring order to the storehouse of their memories.[1] And just as there is something vain about asking who is the greatest poet of all time, or demanding a short list of those poems which must be read or memorized in order for someone to consider himself well-educated, much the same may be said of the historian's works. Different contemporary challenges need to be met by remembering different sorts of past events and per-

---

1. For such a conception of poetry, see T. S. Eliot, "The Social Function of Poetry," in *On Poetry and Poets* (New York: Farrar, Straus and Cudahy, 1957), 7– 9.

sons and to remember them in different ways. From this principle, it does not follow that either poetry or history should be lacking in standards. Thucydides, Tacitus, Bede, and Bossuet are indeed masters and most fitting analogues to Homer, Virgil, Dante, and Racine. Yet just as one reader may be more easily moved to admire the good by a poem of George Herbert than by *Paradise Lost*, so also one may find more light in Gregory's *Life of Benedict*, while another derives more inspiration and encouragement from Thompson's *Francis of Assisi*.[2] What is essential are the principles and the end—that histories are narratives called to exercise right judgment for the sake of the common good of human communities—the means that link them are by their nature manifold.

Viewing the historian's craft as much more than a professional enterprise and as intrinsically ordered to the service of the life of the virtues in community, our reflections upon the practices of the craft and its institutional settings necessarily take the form of an inquiry into the good of historians themselves, of their craft communities, and of the publics that they serve. We offer these reflections, in closing this essay, less as finished judgments and more as proposals to consider.

## To Put on the Mind of Christ

The Christian historian is first and foremost a creature provided with human nature and touched by grace. He is essentially perfected by the beatitudes, the gifts of the Holy Spirit, and by the whole suite of the virtues, both infused and acquired. Within the search for holiness that is the Christian life, craft has an important but dispositive role to play. There is no need here to multiply warnings about how the blinkered pursuit of excellence in a craft can warp the Christian soul.[3] Every

---

2. Augustine Thompson, O.P., *Francis of Assisi: A New Biography* (Ithaca, NY: Cornell University Press, 2012).

3. On the moral dangers of a compartmentalized life, see Alasdair MacIntyre, "Social Structures and their Threats to Moral Agency," *Philosophy* 74 (1999): 311–29. And for a suggestive proposal for the reintegration of academic life, see Reinhard Hütter, "God, the University, and the Missing Link—Wisdom: Reflections on Two Untimely Books," *The Thomist* 73 (2009): 241–77.

thoughtful historian, amateur or professional, wants to avoid the vices of George Eliot's Casaubon.

What needs to be asked and, more crucially, investigated by deeds, is how the historian's craft can be integrated into the Christian pursuit of holiness. How does the historian's consideration of human action translate into a happier and a holier life for him? Perhaps a clue may be had in something Hilaire Belloc once said: in "historical learning" we are given "glimpses of life completed and whole." "And such a vision," he continued, "should be the chief solace of whatever is mortal and cut off imperfectly from fulfillment."[4] What Belloc seems to have meant is that the historian's attention is naturally given over to the rise and fall of nations and families, the birth and death of individuals, the beginnings and the ends of wars and explorations, in a word, to stories that enjoy a certain wholeness or completion. Such wholeness is rarely the direct concern of the scientist or the economist, the statesman or the student of language. In many other fields of intellectual endeavor, analysis is the rule. But the historian, when he picks up his tools of narrative, must always labor to join a beginning to an end.

Here, then, is something particularly philosophical about the historian's craft, a kind of opening to wisdom, for to be wise is to be deeply and perseveringly reflective about ends.

It should indeed be a matter of satisfaction to the historian that his craft has such an inbuilt tendency, for what is surely more striking about the craft from the inside is the way in which it threatens to make its conscientious practitioners unfit for living in the present. To be deep in history—to return to Newman's phrase—is, after all, in the first place to be deep in the past, to be in conversation not with our contemporaries, but with our ancestors. And, as all historians know, the past is elusive. Just as the cabinetmaker must in some sense see the world through grains of wood, or the physician see the marks of health and illness in every person he meets, so also the historian, if he has achieved excellence in his craft, must embrace a certain self-abnegation, by living, in a sense, more in the company of the dead than

---

4.  Hilaire Belloc, *The Old Road* (London: Constable, 1910), 9.

in that of the living. The broader community, however, stands to gain from the historian's voluntary partial ignorance about the present, because it cannot deliberate effectively without understanding how it has come to be in its present state and without knowing what sorts of resources the past has bequeathed to the community in its present hour of need.

Yet the historian's own good requires that he participate in the community not only as a craftsman, but as a full member. And his own pursuit of the good will inevitably call him to reflect upon present challenges and make intelligent decisions about them in whatever mode his membership in the community requires of him. The mental deformation caused by specialization, therefore, needs to be limited by an ordering principle provided by the historian's own pursuit of virtue. The mean that is provided by the integrated Christian life will, to be sure, differ from case to case. Yet the mean will not be found if it is not sought as a necessity. What is needed, and urgently needed, is an ecology of professional life, a sense of order and balance in which the professional tasks of reading, writing, and speaking are yoked to the overall good of the craftsman and of the communities in which he practices. It seems to us that such an ecology will strictly limit the productivity of the historian, asking for fewer articles and monographs and more time for reflection. We would recommend that the historian's reflection challenge a return to first principles and an ascent to the consideration of the last end, which is to say that this reflection should be philosophical and theological. The task of putting on the mind of Christ has its own proper instruments in Sacred Scripture, the writings of the Fathers and Doctors of the Church, and the prayerful consideration of the things of God. The historian, in the search for wisdom, should take the back seat to the Christian. He will, finally, need to find as a model for his craftsmanship someone much more like Bede or Bossuet and much less like the successful stars of the contemporary historical profession.[5]

---

5. For a discussion of Bossuet as this kind of exemplar of Christian intellectual life, see Christopher O. Blum, "The Studiousness of Jacques-Bénigne Bossuet," *Nova et Vetera*, English Edition 8 (2010): 17–32.

### To Pursue the Truth in Charity

Most historians practice their craft within a professional context, but these contexts are not limited to the research university. There are far more historians working in state parks and museums than in major research universities, and countless hundreds of others teach in secondary schools and two- and four-year colleges and write for popular journals of one kind or another. Its function of granting the terminal degree of the Ph.D. may keep the modern university at the top of the historian's field for many decades to come, but already the cracks in the edifice are painfully evident. It is not foreordained that the historian's craft will be renewed by changes in universities before it is renewed by creative initiatives at the grassroots level.

One of the more important opportunities for renewal, it seems to us, is to be found in the decision to make pedagogical reflection central to the historian's craft rather than peripheral. If an historian is essentially always some kind of a teacher, no matter his other roles, then reflection upon the goods that his teaching can offer to the communities of which he is a member promises only to make his craft more valuable. Within schools, museums, military services, religious orders, trade unions and the other sorts of communities he inhabits, the historian provides common premises from which moral arguments can proceed by making the past available to the present. Whether in the form of biographical narratives, descriptions of former laws or customs, the recounting of crucial deeds and decisions, the description of a monument, or a grand narrative of a community or even a whole people, the historian's teaching—written or spoken—should always be a spur to conversation and debate about the good.

The resulting conversation will involve many sorts of voices and perspectives—those provided by literature, philosophy, political theory, theology, and others—but it will be tied together by the common narrative that has brought the community to its current state, and the historians, as custodians of narrative, have the duty to serve their colleagues by keeping that narrative in good order. It seems all too plain that the narrative of Christian civilization has not been kept in good order over the past two generations. The disappearance of core requirements in history and the humanities at Catholic colleges and universities around the country is but one sign of this decay; the emptying out from within of those classes that do remain provides another.

We contend that it is necessary to define the craft of the Catholic historian as the discussion and debate about, and the careful handing on of, the story of Christ's people. To propose such a universal account of the historian's craft is not to insist that every historian be a specialist in everything, and certainly not to suggest that the historian's magnum opus is a multi-volume synthetic history of everything. Instead it is to suggest that our specialization be subordinated to the task of reflecting upon God's work throughout all of time. This must necessarily be a shared work, but to be communal, the sharing cannot be the accidental side-by-side play of children who each have their own square within the sandbox. Rather, common reflection and conversation need to eclipse rival specialized discourses. It is a tall order, but it seems hard to believe that Christian institutions can be satisfied with much less. We fully agree with the observation of James Keating that "a convincing Catholic narration of the rise and fall of Christian cultural and intellectual dominance in the West" seems to be "a necessary condition for the Catholic faith to be a credible animator of academic teaching and learning."[6] In order to animate the search for truth and the quest for the good, such a narrative must be a common good and not the private possession of a specialist. Alasdair MacIntyre has lamented that "we have no institutions through which shared stories can be told dramatically or otherwise to the entire political community."[7] What is necessary at the present hour is to create just such institutions and practices.

---

6. James Keating, "What David Hart's Atheist Delusions Has to Teach Us concerning the Rise and Fall of Christianity's Cultural Dominance in the History of the West," *Nova et Vetera* 9 (2011): 320.

7. Alasdair MacIntyre, "How to Be a North American" (Washington, DC: Federation of State Humanities Councils, 1987), 2.

## Honing the Craftsman's Tools

In addition to their own personal pursuit of wisdom and their service within the broadly speaking academic communities to which they belong, historians also commonly seek a public. It is well that they should do so, and it is only fitting that in an age dominated by various forms of media, that historians find a way to address a variety of publics. Healthy communities make time for their historians to speak, so that they may function as the public voice of the shared memory that binds the community together with its ancestors and offers a patrimony for future generations. Yet at the same time, historians must not wait around for their communities to ask them to speak. As we know all too well, contemporary culture is saturated with expression of one kind or another and will not be able to ask for something that it does not realize that it is lacking.

What we think is needed now are new genres and new modes of expression. The monograph and the classroom lecture will doubtless retain their place in universities—and they should to a degree—but they are even now being undermined by technology. Electronic publication and distance learning will multiply the number of monographs and recorded lectures to the thousands upon thousands over the next decades. Within this surfeit of professional expression, of historians writing for other historians and speaking to their students, what may be overlooked is the need to address different sorts of readers. In the course of this essay, we have already pointed to the sermon, the martyrdom account, the essay, and the papal audience as alternative models to the monograph and the academic lecture. Still other possibilities remain, from historical fiction and drama to the planning of parades, feasts, and public celebrations, the design of monuments, and the telling of stories around campfires. What is essential is that the historian's craft begin in a right understanding of human flourishing, proceed by the making and sharing of good judgments about particular lives and deeds, and be directed toward the future well-being of real human communities. How that craft be practiced will necessarily change with the circumstances in which the craftsman finds himself.

Any fruitful change must begin with an honest recognition of the circumstances in which we find ourselves today. We write as Ph.D. historians trained in the craft—or more properly, the technique—of academic history as practiced for the last hundred years.[8] In short, we have been trained to write monographs. Despite the financial crisis in academic publishing, the monograph remains the standard currency of accreditation and advancement in the profession. This study has suggested the need to question and even to transcend the monograph. Can we as Catholic historians simply say goodbye and walk away? Is there a life after monographs that is not one of intellectual isolation, a retreat to some fideistic ghetto?[9] Thankfully, recent developments in the secular academy suggest that the answer just may be "yes." The production of the "solid monograph" remains the *sine qua non* of professional credibility, yet for at least a generation now a significant number of established scholars have been questioning the basic epistemological assumptions of the conventional monograph. Natalie Zemon Davis's *Return of Martin Guerre* stands as an imaginative reconstruction of the incredible story of a man in early modern France who successfully masquerades as a soldier returning home to his small Pyrenean village after a period of military service. Davis's study not only highlighted the blurred lines between fact and fiction in the account of the French peasant's presentation of himself to the villagers, but in doing so also called attention to the fictions that inevitably shape the historian's presentation of the past to the present.[10] So too, Simon Schama's *Dead Certainties: Unwarranted Speculations,* examines the connections between the deaths of two men, separated by nearly one hundred years, in ways that call into question the reliability of

---

8. For the distinction between craft and technique, see Casey Blake, "Lewis Mumford: Values Over Technique," *Democracy* (Spring 1983): 125–37.

9. For an earlier consideration of this issue, see Christopher Shannon, "After Monographs: A Critique of Christian Scholarship as Professional Practice," in John Fea, Jay Green, and Eric Miller, eds., *Confessing History: Explorations in Christian Faith and the Historian's Vocation* (Notre Dame, IN: University of Notre Dame Press, 2010): 168–86.

10. Natalie Zemon Davis, *The Return of Martin Guerre* (Cambridge, MA: Harvard University Press, 1984).

conventional historical narratives of reconstruction.[11] In these and other works, some leading contemporary scholars show a willingness to detach history from its Victorian roots and incorporate modernist and postmodernist sensibilities which, to be fair, have long since been taken for granted in other sorts of writing. There is, after all, some cause for embarrassment that our contemporary intellectual culture can hold up perspectivalism and fractured narrative as privileged modes of access to "truth" yet consign the pursuit of "truth" in history to clunky, creaky Victorian forms.[12]

Such formal innovations do indeed seem to provide would-be Catholic historians with some narrative breathing room. Still, if they are a way out of Victorian conventions, they are not really something a Catholic historian should want to embrace. As interesting and creative as these works may be, they suffer from the same deficiencies as modernist art; that is, they are ultimately celebrations of the creativity of the author/producer, self-referential exercises in solipsism. We as Catholic historians seek to reach people in order to bring them closer to the truth of Christ. To do this, we must speak in an accessible language and use a "plain style," if you will.[13] Despite the general privileging of modernism in elite intellectual circles, Victorian forms (albeit slightly modernized) continue to dominate popular narrative. Popular history, in particular, tends to be *uber* Victorian—that is, the general reading public seems to have an insatiable appetite for thousand-page biographies of dead presidents.[14] It is unclear how many

---

11. Simon Schama, *Dead Certainties: Unwarranted Speculations* (New York: Vintage, 1992).

12. On this point, see Mark Weiner's provocative essay on legal history, "A History of the Common Law," *Rethinking History* 16 (1) (2012) (*Special Issue: History as Creative Writing* 3): 3–15.

13. Here we invoke the student writing guide of the late historian Christopher Lasch. See his *Plain Style: A Guide to Written English*, Stewart Weaver, ed. (Philadelphia: University of Pennsylvania Press, 2002).

14. On the profession's evaluation of this kind of history, see Sean Wilentz's cutting review of David McCullough's *John Adams*: Sean Wilentz, "America Made Easy: McCullough, Adams, and the Decline of Popular History," *The New Republic* (July 2, 2001).

people who buy such books actually read them, but it is very clear that the sheer size of such works reflects an obsession with the quantitative accumulation of information that undermines the crafting of the tight, dramatic narratives we seek in a renewed Catholic historiography.

Still, some sort of biography does appear to be the most fruitful starting point in terms of narrative form. Biography presents certain challenges, particularly in the way that it often reflects a "great man" view of history and plays into more general modern conceits regarding the centrality of the individual in social life. Seeing the obsession with individuals as a perverted longing for a reflection on Christian personhood, the Catholic historian would shift the biographical narrative from one of individuals striving to control history to persons striving to imitate Christ. In terms of scale and scope of narrative, we would propose a work such as Edmund Morgan's *Puritan Dilemma*.[15] Morgan, one of the great "consensus" historians, writes beautiful, accessible prose shaped by a strong thesis: Winthrop's life understood in terms of his struggle to remain true to the purity of Puritanism without separating from the Church of England. One could very easily argue that Morgan presents a very "consensus" portrait of Winthrop—indeed, in the chapter on "Foreign Affairs," Winthrop almost appears like a prior incarnation of George Kennan. The book endures in part because of Morgan's presentism, his commitment to a strong narrative line intended to serve the needs of his imagined community, the citizens of Cold War America. It was, moreover, part of a series, the Library of American Biography that attempted to provide Cold War Americans with a kind of secular communion of saints who dedicated their lives to the principles of freedom and democracy (a communion broad enough to include Emma Goldman, though now honored with the title, "American Individualist").[16] *The Puritan Dilemma* does not present the whole story of Winthrop, but it does successfully present an important part. No historian today would reduce Winthrop to the

15. Edmund Morgan, *The Puritan Dilemma: The Story of John Winthrop* (Boston: Little, Brown, 1958).

16. John Chalberg, *Emma Goldman: American Individualist* (New York: Harper Collins, 1991).

principle of non-separation, but none would deny that that principle undoubtedly shaped him in profound ways.

The Catholic historian finds a corrective to the dangers of presentism by placing the dramatic narratives of historical persons in the broadest possible contexts: the story of salvation history and the communion of saints over time. Each saint strives to imitate Christ simultaneously in his universality and his particularity. Christ is the universal man, the pattern for all history; yet he is also a first-century Palestinian Jew. Any rendering of the saints as imitators of Christ must be attuned to both those aspects of the model of Christ. History must surely defer to theology and philosophy in treating the universal aspects of Christ, but it may claim the particular as its special area of responsibility.

In *A Theology of History* (1959), Hans Urs von Balthasar argues that the Catholic intellectual tradition, profoundly shaped by Greek thought, has for too long privileged the universal over the particular, timeless essences over historical fact. For Balthasar, Christ's Incarnation broke down the barrier constructed by Greek philosophy and gave a dignity to the material and particular that was distinct to Christianity among all the world religions and philosophical systems.[17] For Balthasar, the saints provide the key to constructing a narrative theology of history that gives full weight to the particularity not simply of persons, but of historical ages:

> Whenever the Spirit takes the Church by surprise with these gifts it is going to be, in the main, by the proclamation of some truth which has far-reaching meaning for the particular age to which it is given, in both Church history and world history. The Spirit meets the burning questions of the age with an utterance that is the key-word, the answer to the riddle. Never in the form of an abstract statement (that being something that it is man's business to draw up); almost always in the form of a new, concrete supernatural mission: the creation of a new saint whose

---

17. Hans Urs von Balthasar, *A Theology of History* (San Francisco: Ignatius Press, 1994), 11, 15, 18.

life is a presentation to his own age of the message that heaven is sending to it, a man who is, here and now, the right and relevant interpretation of the Gospel, who is given to this particular age as its way of approach to the perennial truth of Christ. How else can life be expounded except by living? The saints are tradition at its most living, tradition as the word is meant whenever Scripture speaks of the unfolding of the riches of Christ, and the application to history of the norm which is Christ. Their missions are so exactly the answer from above to the questions from below that their immediate effect is often one of unintelligibility; they are signs to be contradicted in the name of every kind of right-thinking—until the proof of the power is brought forth. Saint Bernard and Saint Francis, Saint Ignatius and Saint Teresa were all of the proofs on that order: they were like volcanoes pouring forth molten fire from the inmost depths of Revelation; they were irrefutable proof, all horizontal tradition notwithstanding, of the vertical presence of the living Kyrios here, now and today.[18]

We cannot truly understand a saint apart from his time, but neither can we understand a time apart from the saints given to us in it. As traditional hagiography often lost the particulars through a somewhat mechanical typology, so a renewed Catholic historiography would give those particulars their full due without losing sight of the saint who is the answer to the burning question of a particular time. Making full use of the scholarly techniques developed over the last hundred years of academic history, a renewed Catholic historiography would nonetheless invert the conventional understanding of text and context: no mere reflection of his times, the saint becomes the context through which we understand the social, cultural, political, economic, and material forces that give shape to the particularity of an age.

This may seem like a lot to pack into a book on the scale of Morgan's *Puritan Dilemma*. Indeed it is. The greatest obstacles, however, may be social rather than technical. Books like *Puritan Dilemma* have

---

18. Ibid., 109–10.

been rare because the profession does not reward them; they are a luxury allowed the rare, odd senior scholar, who is rare and odd because most of his senior colleagues will have had the ability to write such a book beaten out of them by the tenure process. Any renewed sense of history as a craft will depend upon a new form of craft organization. The contemporary professional society is a form of voluntary association appropriate to advancement in a professional world shaped by the large-scale bureaucratic institutions of the state and the market. These institutions served modern society reasonably well through the middle decades of the twentieth century. They were a reasonable response to the tremendous social dislocations brought about by the rise of modern industrial capitalism.[19] For men of Morgan's generation who had experienced World War and the rise of totalitarianism, they appeared to be the last best hope against the self-destruction of Western civilization. Those days are gone, and an honest appraisal of the professional classes must see them for what they are: a class with ideals and interests that often mistakes its interests for ideals. Not all of its achievements have been ignoble, but its most thoughtful exemplars have long since lost faith in its ability to advance anything resembling a humanistic conception of the good life.[20] More pointedly, the crowning institutional achievement of the professional classes, the modern research university, has, at least in the humanities, become little more than a glorified diploma mill certifying students as fit for employment.[21] No, for our craft organization, we must look beyond

---

19. The best account of the rise of the professional classes as an antidote to anarchy remains Robert H. Wiebe, *The Search For Order, 1877–1920* (New York: Hill and Wang, 1967).

20. See, for example, Philip Rieff, *Fellow Teachers* (New York: Harper and Row, 1973) and Christopher Lasch, *The Revolt of the Elites and the Betrayal of Democracy* (New York: W. W. Norton, 1995).

21. See Professor X, *In the Basement of the Ivory Tower: Confessions of an Accidental Academic* (New York: Viking, 2011). Though intended as a critique of humanities education at the lower rungs of the academic ladder, Professor X's argument rang true for many who have tried to impart humanistic learning at the elite level as well. The emerging consensus is that the existing system is entirely dysfunctional for all but those professors and administrators who find themselves in

existing models and back to older ones. We need something like a guild.

The notion of a guild as opposed to a new professional society should commend itself to Catholic historians. There is, after all, a long tradition, going back at least to Leo XIII's *Rerum Novarum*, of appealing to medieval guild models as an antidote to modern anarchy. Sadly, Catholic intellectuals may be the least likely demographic to be drawn to what is after all a medieval Catholic social form. With the exception of figures such as Eamon Duffy and Alasdair MacIntyre, Catholic public intellectuals remain more attached to modernity and its social forms than your average secular intellectual, who we see increasingly drawn to the Eastern religions and environmentalism as an alternative to modern Western materialism. In America, Catholics arrived late to modernity. For them, it still retains some of its luster. The engagement with intellectual modernity often took place within nominally Catholic institutions, thus softening the more alienating aspect of the passage to modernity. Even the rebellious Vatican II generation conducted most of their rebellion within Catholic institutions. The most vocal did not reject the Church so much as fight to control it, to shape its institutions in a particular image.

But there is hope in despair. Even true believers in the so-called "spirit of Vatican II" realize that Catholic institutions have been unable to pass on a strong sense of Catholic identity to contemporary youth. University administrators greeted John Paul II's call for a renewed commitment to the faith in institutions of Catholic higher learning with outrage and indignation at clerical meddling, yet the last ten to fifteen years have seen a dramatic growth in the rise of offices of mission and identity, along with the creation of more than a few programs in Catholic Studies. We see these as encouraging signs, but insist that they are not adequate to the task of a renewed Catholic historiography. For this, we need a guild that is committed to serving

---

very lucrative positions at elite universities. For an alternative educational vision that speaks in part to our notions of craft and the formation of virtuous persons, see Matthew B. Crawford, *Shop Class as Soul Craft: An Inquiry into the Value of Work* (New York: Penguin Press, 2009).

a broader Catholic community outside of the academy first. Even as this guild may draw many of its members from the ranks of trained historians, it will seek recruits prepared to be writers first and scholars second. As writers, they will commit themselves to developing a narrative craft capable of making the Catholic past speak to the Catholic present in such a way as to lead readers to a deeper understanding of the presence of Christ in history.

This distinctly non-academic charism need not, however, exist completely apart from academia. It is our hope that this model of confessional, guild history might appeal to people of different confessions (sacred and secular) who nonetheless seek alternatives to the sterility and plain bad faith of the ossified Victorian forms of scholarly detachment. Were universities to make a place for such an approach to history in their graduate training programs—say under the rubric of a public history orals field—the university might at last live up to its claim to be a meeting place of diverse perspectives rather than an old boy/girl club for modern secular liberals. Once again, on this front, there is cause for hope. The house of secular liberal modernity is, if not divided, at least unsettled. Within the secular consensus, liberal modernists often find themselves in an uncomfortable alliance with more radical post-modernists who want all of the cultural and political freedoms of liberal modernity without any of the philosophical baggage of Enlightenment universalism. Daniel Rodgers, one of the leading U.S. historians writing today, has labeled, and lamented, the rise of postmodernism as an "age of fracture" that has undermined America's ability to work toward achieving the progressive, liberal political goals that once united the nation.[22] Rodgers's account of late–twentieth-century intellectual life reflects more than a little nostalgia for the golden age of consensus liberalism, but his alarm at postmodern fragmentation also reflects the concerns of a communitarian strain

---

22. See Daniel T. Rodgers, *Age of Fracture* (Cambridge, MA: Belknap Press of Harvard University Press, 2011). For a critique of Rodgers's book as a certain kind of liberal confessional history, see Christopher Shannon, "Whose Choir? Which Gospel?: A Response to David R. Stone," *Historically Speaking* XV, no. 4 (September 2011): 31–32.

of liberalism that has the potential to be a fruitful interlocutor with tradition-based history.

Certain pockets of the profession have already shown signs of a new openness to the perspective advanced in this book. In 1998, a group of distinguished historians broke off from the American Historical Association to form a new professional organization, The Historical Society.[23] Though founded to defend "conventional" history against the AHA's drift toward postmodernism and political correctness, its magazine *Historically Speaking* has proven to be a relatively free and open space for raising fundamental questions about the nature of history.[24] So too the recently formed Society for U.S. Intellectual History has provided a space for the revival of a humanistic discourse that takes ideas seriously in a way that the academy has not since perhaps the heyday of consensus liberalism in the 1950s.[25]

Still, we must take these encouraging signs with a grain of caution. Neither communitarianism nor humanism is a universal solvent. There is no common ground that provides a neutral framework for the meeting of disparate traditions. There are, however, common concerns—what is the good life? what does it mean to be human?—that people of good will in different traditions find compelling and enduring. Catholics have historically pursued these questions in dialogue with the various cultures the Church has encountered in the course of its evangelization of the world. The recent pontificates of John Paul II and Benedict XVI have provided exemplary models for a Catholic engagement with Enlightenment modernity. Recently, Jürgen Habermas, one of the most stridently secular defenders of the Enlight-

---

23. Elizabeth Fox-Genovese and Elisabeth Lasch-Quinn, eds., *Reconstructing History: The Emergence of a New Historical Society* (New York: Routledge, 1999).

24. See Christopher Shannon, "From Histories to Traditions: A New Paradigm of Pluralism in the Study of the Past," *Historically Speaking* XII, no. 1 (January 2011): 10–13. The forum includes responses by non-Catholic scholars Elisabeth Lasch-Quinn, Mark Weiner, and Daniel Wickberg.

25. Ironically, this outpost of old-style liberal humanism exists primarily as a blog. See http://us-intellectual-history.blogspot.com/.

enment tradition, has through dialogue come to a greater appreciation of the historical and philosophical insights of the Catholic tradition.[26] True, fruitful dialogue, however, depends on difference. For Catholics to dialogue with modernity and postmodernity, we need to be able to bring something distinct to the conversation. The burden of the argument of this essay has been directed toward renewing a sense of a distinctly Catholic approach to history among Catholic historians. Dialogue also requires risk. In the decades following the Second Vatican Council, Catholics risked much—and lost much—in their engagement with modernity. We have also learned much, and the intellectual achievement of the great contemporary Catholic thinkers we have invoked throughout this essay would have been impossible without the dislocation experienced during the past generation. Drawing on this historical experience, this essay is also an invitation to non-Catholic thinkers to take a risk. As we have tested our truths against the alternatives beyond our tradition, so we ask you to test your truths against the Catholic tradition.

---

26. See, for example, the 2004 exchange between Pope Benedict (then Joseph Ratzinger) and Jürgen Habermas in Jürgen Habermas, Joseph Ratzinger, and Florian Schuller, *The Dialectics of Secularization: On Reason and Religion* (San Francisco: Ignatius Press, 2006), as well as Habermas's later rethinking of his secularism in "Religion in the Public Sphere," *European Journal of Philosophy* 14, no. 1 (April 2006): 1–25.

# Index